U0069570

THE
SPECULATORS
**Based on a True Story of Hong Kong
Movie Script**

First published in July 2020 Hong Kong Book Fair
By Hong Kong Option Class
Room 1026A, KITEC, 1 Trademart Drive, Kowloon Bay, Hong Kong.
e-mail: **thespeculators@hkoptionclass.com.hk**
www.hkoptionclass.com.hk

Copyright © THE SPECULATORS, 2020

All rights whatsoever in this movie script are strictly reserved.
Cannot copy, translate, or perform without the prior written
permission of the publisher.

ISBN : 978-988-78961-2-8

Printed in Hong Kong by
Elegance Printing and Book Binding Co. Ltd.
First print in July 2020

代理經銷：白象文化事業有限公司
地址：401 台中市東區和平街 228 巷 44 號
電話：(04) 2220-8589　傳真：(04) 2220-8505

To My Parents

they worked in the film industry for life

Contents

Preface
by Freeman To Siuhung / 杜蒲鴻

Welcome to THE SPECULATORS where truth is stranger than fiction, love conquers all. And maybe it is the first movie script published in Hong Kong.

In this movie script, my most important contribution was being part of this story because I lived in it. The story described that positive thinking and an optimistic attitude are always the power to re-shape the life better and forever.

Self-Introduction
For more than a decade, I have been writing as a financial columnist for the Hong Kong Economic Journal, a mainstream Chinese newspaper (http://www.hkej.com/). I have also written and published a series of financial books on Futures and Options and as the Principal Instructor running a financial education institute at HK Option Class (http://www.hkoptionclass.com.hk/).

As a licensed individual registered with the Hong Kong Securities and Futures Commission, I work in the Securities and Derivates Department of a listed Chinese Investment Bank. Having built a reputation for excellence, in 2018, the Hong Kong Exchanges (HKEx) presented me the award "Appreciation for a decade of contributions".

The True Story
Because of the reputation and experience, I was invited by Biyu/碧玉 (Lead Actress) and going to Stanley Prison to teach her boyfriend Chris Lin (Lead Actor) how to trade Options. My journey began when I started communicating with Biyu.

In my financial book preface, "Option Long & Short" (in Chinese 《期權 Long & Short》, first version published in 2009), I wrote of an inmate in the Stanley prison numbered 275490 Chris Lin. The true story was, as an Option instructor, I went to Stanley Prison once a week to teach him.

After many visits, I discovered this young man was eager to rebuild his life with the skills he had learned and also impressed with his strong character, I wrote to the Hong Kong Correctional Services Department suggesting an early release of Chris Lin. As a result, in 2013, Chris becomes a free man a few months earlier.

The more visits I made to Stanley Prison, the more I realized that this journey, with a lot of twists and turns of plots, could make an inspirational movie to present the Spirit of Lion Rock in Hong Kong.

This story starts from 1983 before the signing of the Sino-British Joint Declaration, through the date British handover Hong Kong to China at midnight on July 1st 1997, and ends on June 16th 2019, the historical date with 2 million demonstrators clogging Hong Kong streets and chanting, "Five demands! Not one less!".

About Scriptwriting

As chance would have it, I was able to connect with Michael Franklin, a professional screenwriter with over 30 years of experience in the film and production industry. With our shared passion for story-telling, we co-wrote the draft of this script.

In the long creative process, I appreciate my assistants, Frandix Chan and Vivian Luk, they always give help to their utmost.

Movie Script must be in its compact format, but it could be difficult for first-time readers, considering that, Frandix Chan prepared a note "How to read movie scripts" as an aid for movie script reading.

From 1983 to 2019, it is a long journey, to be described by a movie script, and writing errors are always there. As an attentive person, Vivian Luk has done an excellent job of proofreading.

While reading a movie script, the most important thing is to run the scene in your mind, once you get used to it, you will love it. I do think that reading a movie script can help to improve imagination and creation, especially for young people today.

Enjoy your reading!

Freeman To Siuhung / 杜肅鴻
June 2020

How to read movie scripts

A - Formatting

Take a look at the bottom part of page 13 of the script, it contains most of the movie script elements.

---

(1) **INT.** RUN-DOWN GARAGE SERVICE BAYS AND OFFICE - DAY

(2) MECHANICS work on cars. A huge BODYGUARD sits on a stool outside the office door watching everything, and everyone.
(3)

Uncomfortable in this surrounding, and showing it on his face, the 22-year-old Chris approaches the bodyguard.

(4) CHRIS
(5) (unsure of himself)
(6) I heard this is a place where I can borrow money.

The bodyguard pats down Chris for weapons and finding none, nods his head towards the office door.

Knocking on the door he is invited in.

---

(1) Scene Heading. [Left-aligned in ALL-CAPS]
Describes where and when the scene takes place.

(2) Action. [Left-aligned]
Details what is happening and who is taking action.

(3) New character. [ALL-CAPS]
The name of a new character is shown in ALL-CAPS.

(4) Character. [Quadruple-indented in ALL-CAPS]
Names the character who is starting a dialogue.

(5) Parenthetical. [Triple-indented in (parentheses)]
Extra information on how the dialogue is presented.

(6) Dialogue. [Double-indented]
The exact wordings which the character is speaking.

How to read movie scripts

B - Terminology

Special terms and short forms are used in movie scripts. They are listed below by the order of appearance.

FADE IN: — Start of the movie.

EXT. — Exterior, scenes that are filmed outdoors.

Title: — Words to be displayed on the movie screen.

SF — Sound Effect, audible elements of the movie.

(O.S.) — Off-Screen, meaning the character is in the same scene, but not shown when he/she speaks.

INT. — Interior, scenes that are filmed indoors.

(cont'd) — continued, meaning the dialog continues from the same character after some actions.

STORY TELLER — A person, usually never shown on screen, who tells and unfolds the story to the audience.

(V.O.) — Voice Over, meaning the character is not in the same scene location, but his/her voice is being heard.

(MORE) — The dialogue is continued into the next page.

STOCK FOOTAGE: — Pre-recorded video clips, especially for historical events or news broadcasts.

MONTAGE: — A series of short flashes of scenes to deliver condensed information. A fast-forward in time.

Beat. — A momentarily pause for a theatrical effect.

INTERCUT with — Marks the start of a series of actions which alternates quickly between multiple scenes. These actions are usually happening at the same time and progress in multiple locations simultaneously.

FADE OUT. — End of the movie.

Frandix Chan
June 2020

THE SPECULATORS

Based on a True Story of Hong Kong

Story and Creative Consultant by
Freeman To Siuhung/杜嘯鴻

Written by
Michael Franklin and Freeman To

Copyright (c) 2020

1st Edition

e-mail: thespeculators@hkoptionclass.com.hk

THE SPECULATORS
Based on a True Story of Hong Kong

'THE SPECULATORS' is an enduring love story of a prisoner, the story of redemption and salvation of speculators, took place under the Lion Rock of Hong Kong from 1983 to 2019, it is the Big Short and Shaw Shank Redemption, played out on the stage in Hong Kong, the International Finance Center of the World.

FADE IN:

EXT. TAILOR SHOP - RAINY NIGHT (HONG KONG, 1983)

A Benz sits at the curb. The sign above the door reads "Shanghai Tailor Shop", is buffeted by the wind and rain.

Title: "Hong Kong 1983" (Types on screen one letter at a time , SF in sync to letter reveal)

>   BRITISH MAN (O.S.)
>   Having to leave Hong Kong after all
>   these years is bad enough. But not
>   to have you tailor my suits, is
>   tragic.

>   BRITISH WOMAN (O.S.)
>   That's why we bought two.

INT. TAILOR SHOP - RAINY NIGHT (CONTINUOUS)

LIN TAILOR, a Shanghainese in his 30's, stands at the shop doorway with two suit bags and hands them to the British Man who pays for them in U.S. Dollars. His British wife beside him.

>   LIN TAILOR
>   It's been my pleasure to serve you
>   these many years and I'm sad to see
>   you go. I wish you well and safe
>   journey back to Britain.

They shake hands and the couple exit the shop. Lin Tailor locks the door behind them and turns the open sign to closed.

With cash in hand he moves to his small desk at the
back of the shop, opens his desk drawer, removes a
stack of U.S. Dollars, and prepares to count the week's
receipts.

A picture of the family showing his 4-year-old son
CHRIS, and his wife TING TING, sits on the desk with a
small Hong Kong desktop flag beside it.

The happy tailor whistles the tune 'London Bridge Is
Falling Down' as he counts the stack of U.S. Dollars.
He pauses to punch some numbers into a calculator and
is pleased with the results. Picking up the picture of
his family he speaks to it.

                    LIN TAILOR (cont'd)
                 (softly)
          Thank you to all my British
          customers for ordering new suits
          before saying goodbye to Hong Kong.

          You pay me in U.S. and I get 10 Hong
          Kong dollars for each one and the
          market price is already at 9.60.
          Prosperity and a great exchange
          rate, makes me a happy family man.

He continues to count his money.

                    LIN TAILOR (cont'd)
                 (gleefully)
          So happy I'm going to exchange most
          of my H.K. Dollars to U.S. Dollars.
          When Hong Kong comes to be part of
          China in 1997, who knows what will
          happen? For me, U.S. Dollar is the
          best.

                    STORY TELLER (V.O.)
          An old Chinese proverb says, "Coming
          events cast their shadows before
          them." With the British handover of
          Hong Kong to China, the capitalist
          system and way of life that survived
          156 years would change, people are
          preparing.

EXT. TAILOR SHOP - RAINY NIGHT (CONTINUOUS)

Lin Tailor exits the shop, locks the door, and walks
down the street under his umbrella.

>   STORY TELLER (V.O.)
>   As insurance against an uncertain
>   future, many middle-class
>   businessmen sold their Hong Kong
>   dollars to buy U.S. Dollars at a
>   premium.
>
>   Facing both a currency panic and
>   worried about the banks, on October
>   15, 1983 the government announced a
>   fixed rate of 7.80 Hong Kong dollars
>   to one US dollar.
>
>   The overnight drop of nearly twenty
>   percent had a huge negative impact
>   on Hong Kong society. Lin Tailor was
>   one of many victims who suffered a
>   disastrous loss.

INT. LIN TAILOR'S HOME - NIGHT

Lin Tailor sits in a parlor chair reading the financial
section of local newspaper. Losing his temper, he
frightens 4-year-old Chris who wears his festive
Christmas hat.

Chris runs away.

>   STORY TELLER (V.O.)
>   No longer able to take advantage of
>   the high U.S. dollar exchange rate,
>   the middle class lost much of their
>   wealth. Lin Tailor became an angry
>   member of them.

STOCK FOOTAGE: HONG KONG'S HANDOVER FROM UK TO CHINA

Title: "Midnight, July 1, 1997 (13 years later)"

An honor guard approaches a flagstaff flying the UK
flag and lowers it as the British National Anthem --
"God Save the Queen" is played.

The UK flag is replaced with the flag of China and raised as the Chinese National Anthem -- "March of the Volunteers" plays.

> STORY TELLER (V.O.)
> At the stroke of midnight, on July 1st 1997, after 156 years of British rule, Hong Kong was officially returned to Mainland China and a new way of life began. Reaction to the new government caused property values to soar and Lin Tailor's business remained strong.

EXT. BICYCLE PATH NEAR THE SEASHORE - DAY (SUMMER 1997)

Many HAPPY STUDENTS gather along the sea shore and bicycle path enjoying the new life. Hong Kong flag and China flag are separately hanging by the flagpole.

A GUITAR PLAYER is singing an English classical song and drawing others to sing together, some students are organizing a picnic dinner party, girls and boys mingling happily.

CYCLISTS are riding and 18-year-old Chris is out for a stroll along the bike path.

The incessant ringing of a bicycle bell causes him to jump out of the way as the rider, a pretty young girl, BIYU SCARLET SONG, (aka BIYU) also in her late teens, crashes her bike in front of him.

Lying on the ground beside her bicycle, Biyu admonishes Chris.

> BIYU
> Are you deaf, dumb, stupid or all three? I ring and ring my bell and you still don't get out of the way.

> CHRIS
> (tongue in cheek)
> Sorry I was thinking what's the best way to meet a pretty young girl and here you are, right at my feet.

                    BIYU
               (struggling to get up)
          Pig.

                    CHRIS
          It's Chris actually, but if you want
          to call me pig, that's okay. Take my
          hand.

                    BIYU
          My knee hurts. I think I scraped it
          when I fell.

                    CHRIS
               (looking at her knee)
          Scratches. You'll live.

Chris pulls Biyu to her feet as she favors her leg by
leaning on Chris, then he picks up her bike.

                    BIYU
          Thanks. Sorry I called you a pig.

                    CHRIS
          Been called a lot worse. The least I
          can do is to walk you and your bike
          home. You sure can't ride it.

                    BIYU
          It's not far from here and thank you
          Mr. Pig or should I call you
          something else?

                    CHRIS
          Chris please, and you are?

                    BIYU
          My family gave me the name Biyu
          Scarlet Song.

                    CHRIS
          Jasper, the precious stone.

As they walk along the bicycle path.

                    BIYU
               (limping)
          My father may think so but my
          mother, sometimes yes and more
          times, not so precious.

                    CHRIS
          Yes! Parents!

                    BIYU
          Yes! Parents!

They both laugh.

                    CHRIS
          To prove I'm really sorry for
          causing your accident, can I buy you
          dinner? Your choice of restaurant,
          Jasper precious stone.

                    BIYU
          Maybe on the later weekend. I teach
          piano lessons after my nursing
          course during the week, but Saturday
          evenings are free. I like playing
          piano a lot, but my parents want me
          to be a nurse.

                    CHRIS
          I'm studying English at the
          University. My father says I spend
          too much of my allowance money and
          won't advance me more, so I teach
          English to earn extra.

                    BIYU
          Then we are much the same, you and
          me. But before I can say yes to your
          offer, you'll have to pass parental
          inspection. Especially my father's.

                    CHRIS
          And you, my mother's, when the time
          comes.

They look at each other and in unison say.

                    CHRIS & BIYU
          Parents.

INT. TAILOR SHOP - DAY

The once full racks of bolts of cloth are almost bare.
A 'James' stands naked. The cutting table empty.

Lin Tailor sits at his desk counting a few H.K.
dollars. An updated picture of Ting Ting and an 18-
year-old Chris sits beside the original family photo
when Chris was 4.

> STORY TELLER (V.O.)
> For a large number of businessmen,
> the excitement of July 1st 1997 and
> a new Hong Kong government hit rock
> bottom when George Soros attempted
> to break the Hong Kong Dollar's peg
> to U.S. currency, helping to cause
> the Asian financial crisis. The
> business for Lin Tailor, and many
> others went from bad to worse.

Lin Tailor is picking up the updated picture.

> STORY TELLER (V.O.) (cont'd)
> A once proud and prosperous man, Lin
> Taylor was depressed and moody as
> income from his business became
> scarce. Now he was unable to enjoy
> the life he once had.

Studying the picture, his finger traces the family
stopping on the 18-year-old Chris.

> LIN TAILOR
> (to the picture)
> My Hong Kong is no longer. I worry
> the one you inherit will not provide
> the comforts needed to enjoy the
> happy and prosperous life we had
> before.

INT. LIN TAILOR'S HOME - NIGHT

The Lin family is having dinner.

> CHRIS
> Last week I met the girl of my
> dreams by accident.

                TING TING

Does this accident have a name?

                CHRIS

She does. It's Biyu Scarlet Song.
She's a piano teacher and a student
studying nursing at the university.

                LIN TAILOR

And you met her by accident?

                CHRIS

Because of an accident. I was
walking along the bicycle path and
she almost ran me over. Then she
fell to the ground and scraped her
knee.

                TING TING

Good she's studying to be a nurse
then.

                CHRIS

It was just a couple of scratches.
Nothing serious. Mostly hurt her
pride I think.

                LIN TAILOR

When the British left, my pride in
Hong Kong went with them. What we
had before is gone and now we
struggle as a family in so many
ways.

                TING TING

But we're still a family and that's
what matters most.

INT. TAILOR SHOP - EVENING

                CHRIS

But father, as I was the one to
cause the accident, I promised Biyu
I would take her out to dinner to
make amends. Please advance my
allowance just this one time.

                    LIN TAILOR
Business is down and has been for
some time. Have you any idea how
hard it is to make money these days
and all you want to do is spend it.
I work harder now than ever before
for the little income I make, and
you want an advance on your
allowance?

                    CHRIS
Just this once father I promise. It
means so much to me. Never again.

                    LIN TAILOR
How much?

                    CHRIS
Four hundred please father.

                    LIN TAILOR
Four hundred! For a dinner with the
accident girl?

                    CHRIS
Her name is Biyu and you'll meet her
soon I hope.

                    LIN TAILOR
          (angry)
I used to make and sell premium
quality three-piece suits for four
hundred. Now you tell me it buys a
dinner for two? And you're spending
this on a girl you just met?

                    CHRIS
She's special.

                    LIN TAILOR
You're damn right she's special.
Four hundred Hong Kong dollars,
special.

Reaching in his desk drawer he pulls out a small stack
of bills, counts off four hundred and places them on
the top of his desk in front of his son.

                    CHRIS
          I won't ask again.

As Chris reaches for the money, his father's hand comes
down hard covering his son's.

                    LIN TAILOR
          If this accident girl is that
          important to you, together we will
          make you a nice suit to impress her.
          But after school, you will work in
          my shop and learn to tailor. No pay.
          OK?

                    CHRIS
          OK.

The tailor releases his son's hand and Chris puts the
bills in his pocket.

                    LIN TAILOR
          A man must earn his own bread.

Chris nodding happily.

INT. TAILOR SHOP - DAY

Chris gets measured up by his father for his new suit.

MONTAGE: LIN TAILOR MAKING CHRIS'S SUIT

Shots of the tailoring process from start to finish.
Chris, standing in front of the three-panel mirror,
admiring his tailor-made suit. After preening, he gives
his father a big hug.

                    STORY TELLER (V.O.)
          As Chris learned his father's
          business first hand, the bond
          between father and son grew strong.

          Another Chinese proverb states, "A
          gem is not polished without rubbing
          nor a man perfected without trials."
          As years would pass, this proved to
          be true.

INT. UPSCALE RESTAURANT - NIGHT

Chris wearing a shirt, tie and the suit made by his father, and Biyu wearing a slinky dress, enjoy a romantic meal by candle light.

A small gift-wrapped box sits on the table next to Biyu.

> BIYU
> I've never been to such a place as this before. It's beautiful.

> CHRIS
> And you help to make it so.

> BIYU
> You flatter me and I'm not used to that.

> CHRIS
> Well get used to it because it's true. I wasn't kidding when I said I was thinking about meeting a girl, on the bicycle path and there you were at my feet.

> BIYU
> After that comment, it's appropriate I give you my gift.

She hands the box to Chris and smiles as only girls can do.

> BIYU (cont'd)
> I hope you like it?

Chris as he opens his gift.

> CHRIS
> I'm sure I will. It's from you.

Gift unwrapped, Chris removes the lid from the box to reveal.

> CHRIS (cont'd)
> A stuffed pig. How thoughtful of you!

                    BIYU
           (Biyu's smile broadens)
     Yes, I am as you say. Mister pig.

                    CHRIS
           (reaching out to hold
            her hand)
     Yes and playful as well. I like
     that. But remember, who laughs last,
     laughs best.

                    BIYU
     That sounds like a challenge. I hope
     you're up for it. Girls rule you
     know. Let's order, I'm hungry and I
     promised my father I'd be home by
     nine.

Not letting go of Biyu's hand, Chris beckons the WAITER
for menu with his other hand.

                    CHRIS
           Works for me.

EXT. RETAIL STORE DISPLAY WINDOW - MORNING (HONG KONG)

Title: "September 11, 2001"

A CROWD gathers to watch the 9/11 attacks in New York
City on several window display TV's. Caption on TV
screens: "New York LIVE".

Ticker tape runs through screens saying the Hong Kong
market is down. Lin Tailor is part of the crowd.

                    STORY TELLER (V.O.)
           Once again, coming events cast their
           shadows before them. The attack on
           the World Trade Center in New York
           City on September 11, 2001 caused
           markets to fall all over the world.

           As property values declined, Lin
           Tailor's failing business took a
           major hit. Now the proud and once
           successful man, suffered even more.

INT. BIYU'S HOME - AFTERNOON

Listening to Biyu play 'Auld Lang Syne' on her digital piano, a Taiwan flag hangs on one wall. Her father was a former Kuomintang military doctor now living in Hong Kong. Chris appreciates Biyu's performance, eyes full of love.

MONTAGE: CHRIS AND BIYU FALLING IN LOVE

Eating ice cream from a street vendor, riding bikes along the beach front cycle path, holding hands while walking and talking, window shopping, eating pizza, a first kiss, buying Biyu a scarf at the market, bathing Biyu's pet dog.

                    STORY TELLER (V.O.)
          Over the school break, friendship
          blossomed into young love. They
          became inseparable. The two of them
          lived for the next moment they would
          be together again, and parting was
          such sweet sorrow. Then even the
          tutoring money Chris made, ran out.

INT. RUN-DOWN GARAGE SERVICE BAYS AND OFFICE - DAY

MECHANICS work on cars. A huge BODYGUARD sits on a stool outside the office door watching everything, and everyone.

Uncomfortable in this surrounding, and showing it on his face, the 22-year-old Chris approaches the bodyguard.

                    CHRIS
               (unsure of himself)
          I heard this is a place where I can
          borrow money.

The bodyguard pats down Chris for weapons and finding none, nods his head towards the office door.

Knocking on the door he is invited in.

                        AH CHAN
                (from inside the office)
        Come

Opening the door reveals Ah Chan on a sofa flanked by
TWO SEXY YOUNG WOMEN companions. Drug paraphernalia
sits on the sofa table.

                        CHRIS
        Am I in the right place to borrow
        money?

The spaced-out girls giggle.

                        YOUNG WOMAN #1
        You can get more than money if you
        like what you see.

                        YOUNG WOMAN #2
        Double your pleasure, double your
        fun. All it takes is a little cash.

                        CHRIS
                (halting)
        I came, I came to borrow some money.

                        YOUNG WOMAN #1
        No money no honey bright eyes.

                        AH CHAN
        Leave the kid alone. I want to hear
        what he has to say. Business is
        business so you two take a hike. Get
        out.

Young women #1 & #2 exit and as they do, young woman #1
pauses beside Chris and runs her hand down the side of
his face.

                        YOUNG WOMAN #1
        You'd be so nice to come home to.
        Even if it was just for an hour or
        so young stuff.

Young woman #1 exits.

                    AH CHAN
          Toys for big boys. Sometimes they
          drive me crazy. How much and for how
          long?

                    CHRIS
          Can I borrow three thousand for a
          month?

                    AH CHAN
          Most people want 10 thousand. Come
          sit beside me while we get to know
          each other.

Chris sits beside Ah Chan, uncomfortable with what he
sees on the table.

                    AH CHAN (cont'd)
          I usually don't lend such small
          amounts. Even a high interest it's
          hardly worth it.

                    CHRIS
          But I promise to pay you on time,
          every time.

                    AH CHAN
          If you mess up on the payments,
          you'll owe me a favor or two. If you
          mess up on the favors, the big man
          outside my door will come visit you
          and it won't be pretty. Deal?

                    CHRIS
          OK.

Taking a roll of bills from his pocket, Ah Chan peels
off 3,000 H.K. dollars and hands it to Chris.

INT. HONG KONG CITY HALL CONCERT HALL - EVENING

Biyu appreciates the piano performance by Richard
Clayderman. Chris is holding her hand and watching her
enjoying the event.

EXT. CENTRAL AND WESTERN DISTRICT PROMENADE - EVENING
(CONTINUOUS)

After the concert, Chris and Biyu strolled along the
seashore promenade. Biyu is humming the song Mariage
D'Amour they just listened. Her one hand is with Chris
and another is making the music beat. Chris is holding
Biyu, they are kissing each other and embracing
passionately.

INT. GOLD COAST HOTEL SEA-VIEW ROOM - NIGHT

Chris and Biyu make love.

                    STORY TELLER (V.O.)
          On a rainy night in Gold Coast hotel
          room, Chris and Biyu made love for
          the first time. These moments of
          passion changed both of their lives
          forever.

          Unable to pay his debt to Ah Chan,
          little did Chris know the
          consequences would be so grave.

          Chris was forced to become Ah Chan's
          mule. Biyu's disastrous story, had
          yet to be told. That night, their
          separate journeys began. It would
          take many years before reaching
          their destination.

INT. AIRPORT CONCOURSE - NIGHT

A DRUG SNIFFING DOG alerts a BRITISH DRUG INVESTIGATION
BUREAU OFFICER who nods to TWO CHINESE POLICE OFFICERS
to follow Chris.

As Passengers scatter, Chris with his suitcase and
backpack, is chased by 2 police officers through the
airport.

One officer brandishes a baton while the other handles
his ATTACKING DOG.

                    OFFICER #1
                (yelling at the crowd
                 of travelers)
        Out of the way, please.

The chase continues as the young man pays no attention
to the commands of the police.

                    OFFICER #2
                (Releasing the dog)
        Bring him down boy. Get him.

The dog overtakes Chris and bites his leg causing him
to fall to the floor. The suitcase goes flying and
spills open to reveal packages of drugs.

                    OFFICER #1
                (The dog stands guard
                 over Chris)
        You've run your last load of drugs
        into Hong Kong for a very long time.
        Cuff him. I'll call it in.

Officer #2 applies the handcuffs while Officer #1
radios in.

                    OFFICER #1 (cont'd)
        We've got a druggie mule, drugs in
        his backpack and suitcase.

INT. AIRPORT POLICE STATION - NIGHT (CONTINUOUS)

Chris is put in a holding cell. As the cell door
closes,

                    OFFICER #1
        You do the crime, you pay the time.
        Sweet dreams bright eyes. See you in
        court.

Officer #2 runs his nightstick along the bars.

                    OFFICER #2
        Someone tried to get rich using you
        boy and now you'll pay the price.
        How stupid today's kids can be.

Chris sits on his cell bed, head in hands, rocking back and forth and crying.

The light in his cell is switched off leaving only ghostly illumination from down the hall.

> OFFICER #2 (cont'd)
>
> Night.

Footsteps echo down the hall and fade out as the sound of a heavy metal door closes and is latched.

INT. COURTROOM - DAY

Chris, shackled and handcuffed, stands next to his LAWYER in front of the BRITISH JUDGE. In the audience behind him is Lin Tailor, his wife Ting Ting and Biyu. The judge now gives the verdict and passes the sentence.

> JUDGE
> (British accent)
> Young man, before I pass sentence on
> you for the crime of drug
> trafficking, is there anything you
> would like to say?

> CHRIS
> (sheepishly)
> I hurt a lot of people with the
> drugs I carried. People I never met.
> But I hurt the people I love the
> most even more. My mother, my
> father, and the love of my life
> Biyu.

Turning to look at his parents and Biyu, tears in his eyes.

> CHRIS (cont'd)
> For what I've done I am truly sorry.
> I only hope someday you will find it
> in your hearts to forgive me.

Turning back to the Judge.

>   JUDGE
> Chris Lin, considering all the facts
> in this case, for the crime of drug
> smuggling I sentence you to 10 years
> in prison with consideration for
> parole upon good behavior.
>
> Young man, your time in jail should
> be well spent. Learn skills you will
> need for a happy and prosperous
> crime-free life once you are
> released. Take him away.

The gavel smashes down and TWO MARSHALS lead Chris out
of the courtroom. He peers over his shoulder taking one
last look at his family and beloved Biyu. All have
tears in their eyes.

EXT. STANLEY PRISON GATES - MORNING

Title: "Stanley Prison, Fall 2004"

Lin Tailor, Ting Ting and Biyu stand outside the prison
gates waiting to catch a glimpse of Chris as he is
delivered in a prison van.

As the gates open and the van passes through, Chris in
handcuffs, kisses one hand and plants the kiss on the
van window. The three onlookers tear up.

Seeing the prison van entered jail.

>   TING TING
>   (looking at Biyu)
> Biyu, 10 years is too long for you
> to wait for him.

>   BIYU
> My love endures no matter how long
> it takes.

Ting Ting takes Chris's toy pig from her handbag and
hands it to Biyu.

>   TING TING
> Then you deserve this to remind you
> of happier times.

Taking the toy pig from Ting Ting, Biyu and Ting Ting
are crying emotionally as they embrace.

Beat.

Biyu is sobbing with tears but her eyes are slowly
showing her strong personality. She silently puts the
toy pig back to Ting Ting's handbag.

> BIYU
> (sobbing)
> I have a lifetime of happy times to
> remember. Thank you Auntie, but
> please pass this toy pig to Chris
> before his birthday, I know he needs
> it more than I do.

> STORY TELLER (V.O.)
> For Chris and Biyu, redemption would
> take 10 long years to restore their
> lives. Only then would a new life
> begin for both of them.

INT. CHRIS'S PRISON CELL - NIGHT

Chris reads his finished letter to Biyu aloud.

> CHRIS
> (reading his letter)
> Dear sweet Biyu. My thoughts and
> prayers reach out to you as they
> have so many times before. Without
> the memories of our lives when we
> were together, I think I would go
> insane.
>
> Life here is not easy but thinking
> of you makes it more bearable. Many
> more days will come before I am free
> and it's because of this, I urge you
> to find another. Someone who will
> treat you better than I can from in
> here.

INT. BIYU'S BEDROOM - NIGHT

Biyu reads the rest of the letter to herself.

                         BIYU
          You deserve to have a real life. One
          I can't give you because I am here,
          and you are there. I will be both
          sad and happy for you, when you do.

          I love you more than life itself.
          'Jasper precious stone'.

Biyu takes a breath.

                         BIYU (cont'd)
          But it's time for you to move on
          without me. Time to start your new
          life. Chris.

INT. PRISON CANTEEN - DINNER TIME

Chris, meal tray in hand, is looking for a seat but
nobody is willing to let him sits aside. He can only
find a seat next to the kitchen waste bin. While he is
sitting down and watching the meal tray.

                         CHRIS
                       (to himself)
          Will this kind of life be lasting
          for a decade?

He throws the uneaten into the bin and return the meal
tray to the table, then walks alone to the exercise
yard, it is getting dark.

EXT. PRISON EXERCISE YARD - DUSK

Chris walks alone in the yard as the sound of happy
memories echo in his head.

                         BIYU (REPRISE)
          Are you deaf, dumb, stupid or all
          three?

                         CHRIS (REPRISE)
          I was thinking what's the best way
          to meet a pretty young girl and here
          you are, right at my feet.

                    BIYU (REPRISE)
Pig.

                    CHRIS (REPRISE)
Four hundred dollars Father. She's
special.

                    LIN TAILOR (REPRISE)
You're damn right she's special.
Four hundred Hong Kong dollars
special!

                    CHRIS (REPRISE)
A stuffed pig. How thoughtful of
you!

                    BIYU (REPRISE)
Yes, I am as you say. Mister pig.

INT. BIYU'S BEDROOM - DAY

Sitting on the edge of her bed she looks at the
markings on a home pregnancy kit that reveal she's
pregnant. The rest of the kit is visible on her bedside
table.

INT. BIYU'S BEDROOM - DAY (CONTINUOUS)

BIYU'S PARENT, DR. SONG and MRS. SONG, going in and out
of her bedroom and blaming.

                    MRS. SONG
How could you do this to your father
who has worked so hard to give you a
good life?

                    DR. SONG
It is really a shame! Now we have to
live with your shame.

                    MRS. SONG
We need to find a way to save face
for all of us before it's too late.

> DR. SONG
> You will leave for Taiwan to live
> with your Aunt, and to have an
> abortion as soon as possible.

As Dr. Song storms out, Biyu breaks down in tears.

> BIYU
> (to herself)
> If I'm to mother a child with no
> father, love by one is not as good
> as love by two. In today's world it
> will be difficult. But so will
> having the abortion my parents want.
> My path to choose is not yet clear.

INT. PRISON VISITING ROOM - DAY

Biyu enters the room and finds Chris seated on the
other side of the glass divider. Using the phones to
communicate, other inmates talk with their families.

Chris beams at the sight of Biyu who has taken time to
look her best. As she sits and picks up the receiver.

> CHRIS
> Hello my love. Still as beautiful as
> ever.

> BIYU
> (smiling)
> And you as flattering as ever. Your
> words warm my heart. And that makes
> me happy.

> CHRIS
> Life here is really not easy, how
> about you?

> BIYU
> Bad and unhappy as well.

> CHRIS
> Say it isn't so my love.

>   BIYU
> It is. My parents are sending me to
> Taiwan to live with relatives. They
> think I should have a new life.

>   CHRIS
> Happy and sad. I said it before, and
> I'll say it again. I'll be happy for
> you and sad for me.

Tearing up, Biyu drops the phone receiver, takes one
look at Chris, kisses her hand and plants it on the
divider glass in front of her. In real tears, she
stands up, walking away, turns her head for the last
look at Chris and leaving the room.

A dejected Chris places his hand on the glass to cover
where Biyu's once was.

INT. BIYU'S BEDROOM - EVENING

Taking a break from packing her suitcase, Biyu is
writing a birthday card for Chris.

>   STORY TELLER (V.O.)
> Unlike Romeo and Juliet these lovers
> were not to be separated by death,
> but by life. Both imprisoned in
> their own form.

> Once her body adjusted to the
> abortion, the plan was for relatives
> in Taiwan to find her another man.

> Biyu never told Chris she was
> pregnant.

After writing, Biyu sprays perfume on the birthday card
and put it inside the envelope. And sets it on her
bedside table beside a picture of a happy Chris and
Biyu together.

Biyu sadly playing a few first bars of a song of Romeo
and Juliet.

INT. PRISON HALLWAY OUTSIDE CHRIS'S CELL - NIGHT

A PRISON GUARD bangs his night stick on the bars.

> PRISON GUARD
> Your mum left this box for you
> today.

> CHRIS
> Oh, thank you Sir.

Chris takes the box and opens it and smiles.

> PRISON GUARD
> We had to open it and check the
> contents. You are really a big boy,
> aren't you?

> CHRIS
> (answering the Guard)
> Yes, I truly am!

> PRISON GUARD
> Also we received post letter,
> because of the smell, we also opened
> it and check.

> CHRIS
> Oh, really? thank you again, Sir.

Chris takes the post letter, smells and with surprising
eyes.

> CHRIS (cont'd)
> Oh, my love.

Sitting on the edge of the bed, Chris takes the toy pig
out from the box and kisses it.

> CHRIS
> Love you, my precious stone, that is
> the only pleasure I have here.

Chris smells and kisses the letter again and open. It
is a birthday card, he is reading to himself.

> CHRIS
> "I hope by now you have received my
> toy pig from your Mum.
> (MORE)

> CHRIS (cont'd)
> Yes, I am leaving for Taiwan, but as
> I said it is not my will.

> BIYU (V.O.)
> My answer is no! No, I will not be
> looking for another and yes, I will
> be waiting for you no matter how
> long it takes or how difficult my
> life will be without you.

Chris stands up.

> BIYU (V.O.) (cont'd)
> We will be together again. This is
> my words to you, my love. Biyu".

Chris smells and kisses the birthday card once again
and puts together with the toy pig.

It becomes his shrine. Reclining on the bunk, his eyes
moisten as he thinks of the girl he left behind.

INT. BIYU'S HOME - DAY

Biyu sits at her digital piano, tears in her eyes
playing the a few last bars of a song of Romeo and
Juliet. The picture of a happy Chris and Biyu together
sits on the top of the piano. Her packed suitcase on
the floor beside her.

EXT. BIYU'S HOME - DAY

A taxi waits at the curb, Biyu's father, Dr. Song,
follows with her small suitcase, places it in the trunk
while Biyu slides into the back seat of the taxi. He
then closes the door.

> DR. SONG
> Years from now you'll thank us for
> this. It's for the best. You need to
> meet an eligible young man and your
> Auntie has promised to arrange all.

> BIYU
> (through tears)
> There are so many thoughts in my
> mind right now I don't know what I'm
> going to do. But Father, if I need
> help, I'll call you.

EXT. TAIWAN AIRPORT - DAY (FALL 2004)

Customs, Immigration Arrivals level as Biyu checks in.

> STORY TELLER (V.O.)
> The less-than-two-hour flight from
> Hong Kong to Taipei was not long
> enough for Biyu to decide what she
> should do.

Exiting the terminal, Biyu hails a cab.

> STORY TELLER (V.O.) (cont'd)
> Should she follow her heart and defy
> her parents or bend to their will,
> have an abortion, and seek another
> man. No matter her choice, the pain
> on her face for making the right
> decision was obvious.

EXT. TAIWAN TRI-SERVICE GENERAL HOSPITAL ENTRANCE - DAY

Biyu drops down from a taxi, her belly is starting to
show. With light suitcase in hand, she enters the
hospital.

> STORY TELLER (V.O.)
> The ultra-sound check was the first
> stop on her Taiwan journey. It would
> take many years before Biyu would
> return to Hong Kong and finally be
> at peace with her decision.

INT. TAIWAN TRI-SERVICE GENERAL HOSPITAL MATERNITY
WARD - DAY

With signage on the wall to identify this is Maternity
Ward, A TAIWAN NURSE conducts an ultra-sound on Biyu's
stomach and reports.

                    TAIWAN NURSE
Congratulations. You're having a
baby boy. If you like I can make a
copy of the ultra sound for you to
keep as a memory of this happy day.

                    BIYU
            (stoic in her reaction)
Thanks. I pray someday it will be a
happy day.

                    TAIWAN NURSE
Did you want a girl instead of a
boy?

                    BIYU
As long as the baby is healthy, it
doesn't matter.

                    TAIWAN NURSE
Most mothers-to-be say the same
thing. They're happy to become a
mother.

                    BIYU
So am I, but it's complicated.

                    TAIWAN NURSE
Dear lady, this is the best hospital
in Taiwan. We deliver thousands of
babies each year. There's nothing
complicated about that.

                    BIYU
It's not about the hospital is about
me. A copy please just in case.

EXT. PRISON EXERCISE YARD - DAY (2006)

Chris is drawn to the sound of a harmonica playing Auld
Lang Syne by OLIVER, who sits alone against a wall in
the yard.

                    CHRIS
Hi, your music reminds me of someone
special. Someone I haven't seen much
of since I've been in this shit
hole.

                    OLIVER
               (British accent)
Shit hole it is. Surrounded by steel
bars, doors, midnight bed checks and
all the lousy food you can't eat.
Music helps me to forget. Looks like
I'll be playing it a lot in here.

                    CHRIS
               (chuckling)
You'll get used to it. You're new
here. How so?

                    OLIVER
Got caught forging financial
documents. Now this is my home for
the next three years. And what about
you?

                    CHRIS
I smuggled drugs to pay off some
debts.
               (shaking hands with
                Oliver)
Chris is the name. Welcome aboard.

                    OLIVER
Oliver, as in Oliver Twist.

                    CHRIS
But not an orphan working for an
undertaker!

                    OLIVER
A man of letters. I'm impressed.

                    CHRIS
I majored in English at university
and then was an English tutor. My
father has a tailor shop, I helped
him sometimes.

                    OLIVER
How about smuggling drugs?

                    CHRIS
               (smiling)
Don't mention it.

OLIVER
In the financial market, when you
understand the risk, there is no
risk. But in the real life, if it's
a risk, it must be so.

CHRIS
No idea what you said.

OLIVER
I used to trade a market derivative
called Options. It can be risky, but
once you understand how it works,
you can make money by avoiding the
risk.

CHRIS
Risky, it can be risky but if you
avoid the risk you can make money. I
feel so much better now.

OLIVER
When I forged that document, I took
a risk and made handsome money. Then
I got caught, and now I pay the
price.

CHRIS
My price is 10 years here to pay my
stupid.

Oliver puts the harmonica back in his pocket.

OLIVER
If I kept on trading options instead
of forging documents, I could make
money a lot but slowly. Being stupid
also to make quick money and now I
will stay here for 3 years.

CHRIS
How is it possible that by trading
options you can make money so
easily?

OLIVER
Not easy at all! But it is more than
worth to learn in the financial
market.
(MORE)

> OLIVER (cont'd)
> It needs some talent, a lot of
> knowledge, and a bit of luck to be a
> successful trader.

> CHRIS
> A thinking man's game like chess. I
> like that. Maybe you can teach me
> how to trade.

> OLIVER
> Not having much to do for the next
> few years, why not if you are
> interested. And you teach me how to
> speak better Chinese. Deal?

> CHRIS
> Deal! It surely makes it easier to
> get a Chinese girlfriend if you do.

> OLIVER
> Congratulations. You just made your
> first trade.

EXT. PRISON EXERCISE YARD - DAY

An impatient Oliver plays a riff on his harmonica while
he waits for Chris's arrival.

> OLIVER
> Good one of us is an early riser. I
> hate it when people are late.

Oliver finishes writing a traditional option trading
diagram on paper and hands it to Chris who listens
intently and scribbles notes.

> OLIVER
> Let's get started. An Option is a
> time sensitive finance tool, that
> loses time value once you are
> holding it. To be a good trader,
> timing is always critical.

> CHRIS
> Late no more. I don't want to make
> my teacher mad at me.

                    OLIVER
An option is a contract with
selectable time and strike price.
The buyer pays for the right to buy
or to sell but without obligation,
and seller received the money with
obligation to sell or to buy. People
use options for income, to
speculate, and to hedge risk.

                    CHRIS
What language are you speaking?

                    OLIVER
The language of business. Of how to
make real money. You want to earn
you have to learn!

                    CHRIS
I want both.

                    OLIVER
Then start by learning how to
generate income and how to speculate
to make cash flow. Once your size is
big enough then we can move on to
hedge.

A GUARD appears, the time is up.

Chris grabs the paper and his notes and leaves with
Oliver.

EXT. PRISON EXERCISE YARD - DAY

                    CHRIS
Your harmonica playing, is that
something you do a lot?

                    OLIVER
Locking in here for 3 years, I'll
play it every chance I get. It makes
surviving in this hell hole easier
to take.

Taking the harmonica from his pocket.

OLIVER (cont'd)
I'll give you a little harmonica
history. This tiny instrument has
been soothing people's souls close
to 200 years. Matthias Hohner is the
father of the modern-day harmonica.

CHRIS
Amazing you can get so many sounds
from something that small. Would you
play Red River Valley for me?

OLIVER
Sure!

Chris closes his eyes and thinks of Biyu while Oliver
plays.

OLIVER (cont'd)
Some special meaning attached to
that old American cowboy love song?
Like a girlfriend maybe?

CHRIS
Yes, my girlfriend. I miss her a
lot. Especially at night when I'm
lying in my cell. She plays piano
and if I can play harmonica with
her, that would be great.

OLIVER
It's all about breathing in and out.
Inhale and exhale. Part of the
technique used to express your
feelings through music.

Oliver demonstrates the inhale and exhale with his
harmonica.

OLIVER (cont'd)
It is an emotional magnet and the
reason I played Auld Lang Syne in
the yard. It brought you to me, and
here we are.

CHRIS
Then I want to learn Harmonica, too.

Oliver smiles.

INT. PRISON COMMON AREA - DAY

Oliver prepares a few pages of lessons. The harmonica
sits aside.

>   OLIVER
>   So what's it to be today. Option
>   Trading or harmonica?

>   CHRIS
>   Music maestro, please. Let's start
>   there. If I can learn Options
>   trading and Harmonica, I'll be a
>   happy man, I've got lots of time to
>   do both.

Oliver plays an extended riff to show off.

>   OLIVER
>   The first thing to learn about
>   playing the harmonica is to get a
>   good understanding of the song's
>   score. If you can't do that, then
>   nothing else matters.

Oliver demonstrates.

>   CHRIS
>   Noted. You need to be able to read
>   the song's score.

>   OLIVER
>   Then learn the technique of inhaling
>   and exhaling and how they make
>   different sounds. Like learning
>   option trading, it all takes time.

>   CHRIS
>   By the time I'm out of here, I'll be
>   an expert in both I hope.

>   OLIVER
>   Then Mr. Expert to be, let's start
>   with Options. Listed Options can be
>   divided into two categories. Index
>   Options and Stock Options. They're
>   from the same family but the trading
>   strategy for both is quite
>   different.

                         CHRIS
          Hold on a minute while I make my
          notes. A good set makes nighttime
          studying a whole lot easier.

Chris scribbles his notes while Oliver waits.

                         CHRIS (cont'd)
          Done. Now what professor Oliver?

                         OLIVER
          Options are just a tool to use, and
          to use it well, you must keep
          studying the market. Calculate the
          possible volatility and only then,
          plan your strategy.

                         CHRIS
          Sounds like the chess game of
          business.

                         OLIVER
          Trust me. It's a jungle out there.
          Only smart people willing to take a
          chance are going to survive.

                         CHRIS
          No wonder people make so much money
          in finance trading.

                         OLIVER
          Master it and enjoy the rewards.

                         CHRIS
          Sure, master it, I will.

INT. CHRIS'S PRISON CELL - NIGHT

Chris studies his daily lesson.

                         STORY TELLER (V.O.)
          The end of the day was just a
          momentary pause in Chris's education
          as he reviewed all the lessons of
          the week. He was a determined man.

INT. PRISON VISITING ROOM - DAY (FALL 2008)

Biyu walks in the visiting room with her slimmer body
and sitting at the glass divider and waiting for Chris.

>   STORY TELLER (V.O.)
>   After a few years of banishment in
>   Taiwan, Biyu returned to Hong Kong.
>   The couple of lovers is anxious to
>   see each other.

Chris comes and looking at Biyu

Beat.

They quickly pick up the receiver but say nothing, just
looking at each other.

>   CHRIS
>   As beautiful as ever. Time has been
>   good to you, Jasper my precious
>   stone. Could you stand up and turn
>   around? I want to see you in full.

Biyu smiles, standing up and turning around.

>   CHRIS (cont'd)
>   My dear, the only disappointment is
>   that I cannot hold you in my arms. I
>   long for that.

>   BIYU
>   Soon my love. We'll be together like
>   before. I promise!

Beat.

>   BIYU (cont'd)
>   You are matured and more masculine,
>   my love, I have a lot to tell you,
>   how about you?

>   CHRIS
>   And I have lots to tell you as well
>   even some good news.

>   BIYU
>   Oh, really, you first please.

                    CHRIS
Yes, I'm learning how to be an
Options Trader so when I get out of
here, I can make a decent and honest
living.

                    BIYU
Amazing! Just like the judge told
you?

                    CHRIS
Yes. Just as what she said. I met
another prisoner who has many years
of experiences in the finance
business. He has been teaching me
what he knows.

                    BIYU
Wonderful, so no more drugs?

                    CHRIS
Surely No! This is a real job that
can make handsome money.

                    BIYU
How you met the guy here?

                    CHRIS
Yes, he is a Hong Kong born
Australian. In the exercise yard, I
heard him playing Auld Lang Syne on
his harmonica. It made me think of
you playing the piano. So I
introduced myself and now we meet
every morning after breakfast.

                    BIYU
So happy to know that. I think my
news is as good as yours.

                    CHRIS
Say quickly, let me know you will
not return to Taiwan.

                    BIYU
Yes! My father helped me to find a
nurse job in Hong Kong and I still
want to be a piano teacher.
                    (MORE)

                    BIYU (cont'd)
          The best is now I am staying here
          and waiting for your release.

Happy Chris kisses the receiver and made Biyu very
happy also.

INT. PRISON COMMON AREA - DAY (FALL 2008)

Oliver shows to Chris a collection of newspapers.

Oliver and Chris continue the lessons on using Options
to make money in a bearish market. On the paper is a
drawing of the Hang Seng Index showing a high of 31,958
in Nov 2007 and a low of 10,676 in Oct 2008.

                    OLIVER
          Here's what it looked like in the
          newspaper. In Options trade, if you
          keep the Long Put positions on index
          futures with limited risk, you can
          make an unbelievable amount of
          money.

                    CHRIS
          Oh, that's what it's all about?

                    OLIVER
          Pay attention to Wall Street, it has
          about 55% of the global finance
          market. It's there you'll find lots
          of cases worth studying.

                    CHRIS
          Good to know. But my sense tells me
          that it is some feeling in the gut
          and not always to do with the
          numbers.

                    OLIVER
          Yes, of course, if it was easy, they
          already gave the job to the others.

                    STORY TELLER (V.O.)
          Making his points, and using the
          financial section of the newspaper,
          Oliver taught Chris how to study
          Wall Street.

                    (MORE)

> STORY TELLER (V.O.) (cont'd)
> From the learning results, Chris was
> hooked, trading options could be his
> career. It also cemented a life-long
> friendship between teacher and
> student.
>
> And Biyu returned from Taiwan, and
> as an outside partner to give help,
> Chris and Oliver, they started a
> small money option trade.

INT. HALLWAY OUTSIDE PRISON OFFICE - DAY (SPRING 2009)

Oliver exits the office and closes the door behind him.
He takes his release letter and is so happy, he kisses
it and speak to himself.

> OLIVER
> I'm out of here. Done like dinner.
> Paid the check and on my way.

INT. PRISON OFFICE - DAY

Back in civilian clothes, Oliver says goodbye to Chris.
He hands Chris his harmonica and a copy of "Free to
Choose".

> OLIVER
> Whenever I was feeling low, I used
> my harmonica and this book to lift
> my spirits. This book is Milton
> Friedman's works, who is the Nobel
> Prize Winner in Economics 1976. I
> managed to survive and you will too.
> Take care my friend.

They embrace. Without another word, Oliver turns and
walks out of the room leaving the poor Chris alone.

> STORY TELLER (V.O.)
> Released, Oliver gave his harmonica
> and his copy of "Free to Choose" to
> Chris. Over the remaining years of
> Chris's sentence, he learns to play
> it well and reads "Free to Choose"
> over and over again.

INT. HONG KONG OPTION CLASS CLASSROOM - DAY (SUMMER 2009)

FREEMAN TO stands at a white board studying option strikes quotation.

The desk phone rings, a phone conversation starts.

>   FREEMAN
>   Option class. Freeman To speaking.
>   How may I help you?

>   BIYU (V.O.)
>   Dear To Sir, I researched your books
>   and newspaper articles and I believe
>   you are the best person to teach
>   Option Trading in Hong Kong.

>   FREEMAN
>   Oh, thank you for the kind words. If
>   it is your interest, you may take a
>   course, the new time table uploaded
>   yesterday.

>   BIYU (V.O.)
>   Yes, I know, but do you have one-on-
>   one lessons?

>   FREEMAN
>   I do have private lessons and the
>   time could be arranged to fit your
>   schedule. But why do you need
>   expensive private lessons? Are you
>   leaving Hong Kong soon?

>   BIYU (V.O.)
>   No, I am living here. But I need to
>   learn from you quickly so I can
>   teach someone else.

Beat.

>   FREEMAN
>   I can teach you how to be an Option
>   trader, but wonder if I can teach
>   you to be an Option teacher.
>
>   It's better you and your student
>   attend the private lesson together.
>   (MORE)

                    FREEMAN (cont'd)
You just pay one person's charge is
fine.

                    BIYU (V.O.)
Yes, thank you, but I wish it was
that easy.

                    FREEMAN
To take a course is that difficult?

                    BIYU (V.O.)
OK, let me say straight, the student
is my boyfriend and now in Stanley
Prison. His option teacher was a
fellow inmate, he learns from this
teacher in the jail till the teacher
was released. Now he is anxious to
continue his Option learning.

                    FREEMAN
Oh, I see, it is very interesting.

                    BIYU (V.O.)
So, I wish to learn from you quickly
and then go to jail to teach him. Of
course, if you could go to jail to
teach him directly, it will be
wonderful. Your reputation says that
should be you, To Sir.

                    FREEMAN
I'm flattered you would consider me
for such an undertaking. I need to
think how this could work. Give me a
couple of days, my assistant will
call you back.

                    BIYU (V.O.)
Thank you so much! To Sir.

Hanging up the phone, Freeman says to himself,

                    FREEMAN
A prisoner in Stanley Prison wants
to be an Option Trader. Amazing!
What a challenge!

EXT. PRISON EXERCISE YARD - DAY

Up against the same wall Oliver used to play Auld Lang
Syne, Chris practises playing the harmonica. It does
not sound like music.

TWO BULLIES are approaching.

> BULLY #1
> Hey you noise maker, where's the big
> guy that knows how to play that
> thing?

> BULLY #2
> Your buddy the Aussie.

> CHRIS
> Released yesterday. You got a
> problem with that?

> BULLY #1
> No sweet cheeks, we got a problem
> with you and your noise machine.

Sensing confrontation, Chris stands.

> CHRIS
> Really? And what would that be.

> BULLY #2
> Give the noise machine to me!

Chris is holding the harmonica on his chest tightly.

> CHRIS
> What's that got to do with you?

Bully #1 hits Chris's face and Bully #2 lunges at Chris
knocking him down and tries to grab the harmonica, but
Chris is still tightly keeping the harmonica on his
chest and lying on the ground. The bullies kick a
helpless Chris.

As whistles sound and GUARDS come running, Chris lies
motionless, harmonica still on his hands.

Guards arrive, break up the fight and take the two
bullies away.

                    CHRIS (cont'd)
                 (stand up and defiant)
          You picked the wrong guy to fuck
          with.

EXT/INT. TAILOR SHOP - DAY (YEARS LATER)

A taxi cab stops in front and Biyu exits, looking slim
and trim. Entering the shop, the automatic doorbell
sounds. The once thriving business is run-down now. A
separating curtain opens to reveal Shanghai Lin
Tailor's wife Ting Ting.

                    TING TING
          May I help you?

                    BIYU
          It's me, Biyu, it's been years! I'm
          back from Taiwan and there are a lot
          I want to tell you. May I come in?

Hearing the doorbell, from behind the curtain, Lin
Tailor asks,

                    LIN TAILOR (O.S.)
          Who is it?

                    TING TING
          Father, it's Biyu, she is back from
          Taiwan.

Shanghai Lin Tailor takes off his glasses and looks
Biyu up and down as if she is a ghost. In many ways,
she is.

                    LIN TAILOR
          Oh, Biyu, please sit down, how about
          you in these years? After the prison
          gates, I don't remember seeing you
          until now.

                    BIYU
          Yes, there are many reasons why my
          parents banished me to live in
          Taiwan. Even Chris doesn't know what
          happened. I come to see you with
          some good news.

> TING TING

Good news? I'm about to get some
tea. Please wait to tell me the
details, I want to hear every word.

> BIYU

Yes, some good news. It's been many
years, life is not easy, but finally
I got it.

Biyu received a cup of tea from Ting Ting.

> BIYU (cont'd)

After all these years, Chris and I
are still in love. I read it in his
letters to me and I'm sure he reads
it in mine. With years apart, he is
still the sunshine in my life.
> (takes a sip of tea)

I visited Chris last week, and we
plan to get married after his
release.

> TING TING

Oh! It really is the best news if
your plan is to get married. Today
is a super good day.
> (pours some tea for
> Biyu)

Continue, please.

> BIYU

I'm here to bring you more good
messages. In jail, Chris met a
fellow prisoner who's been teaching
him how to make money on the stock
market by trading options, three of
us have started some small money
trading, so far so good.

> LIN TAILOR

And he will continue this business
once he gets out of prison?

> BIYU

Yes, by then it will be even more
profitable.
> (MORE)

> BIYU (cont'd)
> When his prisoner teacher was
> released, I have searched for
> another professional to continue
> Chris's studies.

Biyu shows Freeman's articles and a book to Lin Tailor.

> BIYU (cont'd)
> I used the profit from our small
> money trading to invite this Option
> Instructor.

> TING TING
> And our son will be a businessman
> then?

> BIYU
> Yes, he surely will be. The new
> instructor will once a week visiting
> the jail for the 30 minutes allowed.
> He's a columnist who has been
> writing for a mainstream Hong Kong
> newspaper for 5 years, and a man
> with lots of financial knowledge and
> experience. His name is Freeman To.

> LIN TAILOR
> I don't know too much about finance,
> just know this business is using
> money to make money, smart guys make
> a lot.

> I have not much money left now but I
> am interested to put some money for
> Chris to trade.

> BIYU
> Oh really? Chris must be happy to
> have you as his first client.

> LIN TAILOR
> And I'll be happy to see my son as a
> man who earns his own bread.

INT. STANLEY PRISON MAIN ENTRANCE - DAY (SUMMER 2009)

The new Options Instructor Freeman To gets checked out
by curious guards as he passes through security.

STORY TELLER (V.O.)
Hearing this new visitor has a
reputation as a Financial Option
Instructor and not knowing what that
is, all guards are looking at
Freeman and wonder why he has come
to Stanley Prison.

INT. PRISON VISITING ROOM - DAY (SUMMER)

On the opposite sides of the glass, phone receivers in
hand, Chris and his new instructor Freeman To, have
their first lesson.

FREEMAN
My name is Freeman To. Biyu has
invited me to be your option
instructor.

CHRIS
I'm Chris Lin, thank you To Sir, I'm
so grateful for you coming here.
Biyu is my fiancee and she's always
helping me.

Freeman smiles.

CHRIS (cont'd)
I've been saving your articles in
the Hong Kong Economic Journal for
years, and have quite a collection.

Chris shows a stack of papers.

Freeman, surprised and moved by Chris's collection,
gives Chris a smile and says to himself, "What a smart
guy!".

FREEMAN
I was told from Biyu about your
inmate teacher. You must be a
serious student and want to continue
your learning.

                    CHRIS
          Yes, my previous teacher said that
          if you want to earn, you have to
          learn, and Option is more than worth
          to learn.

                    FREEMAN
          Great! Then it's good to start.

Freeman holds the New Concept of 4-way Cycle Option
graph up against the glass for Chris to see.

                    FREEMAN (cont'd)
          First of all, we need to change the
          existing thinking of the stock
          market has only two directions, rise
          and fall, but Cycle Option adds two
          more directions, limited rise and
          limited fall, making a total of four
          directions.

From the other side of the glass, Chris takes notes and
draws a picture of the chart seriously.

INT. CHRIS'S PRISON CELL - NIGHT

Chris studies the hand drawn Cycle Option chart and the
many lessons he has scribbled out during Freeman's
instruction sessions. There is paper everywhere.

                    STORY TELLER (V.O.)
          The half-hour time limit rule for
          visitation every week was never
          enough for the instructor and the
          note taking student. They could have
          gone on for hours.

INT. STANLEY PRISON MAIN ENTRANCE - DAY (WINTER 2009)

Freeman taking off the coat and passing through the
security check.

                    STORY TELLER (V.O.)
          Much to the surprise of the prison
          guards, Freeman visits his student
          every week. After a few months, the
          guards give him friendly smiles.
                    (MORE)

STORY TELLER (V.O.) (cont'd)

They had never experienced anyone
dedicated to the salvation of a
prisoner before.

INT. PRISON VISITING ROOM - DAY

Freeman enters the Visiting Room carrying his winter
coat, and a book in his hand. He takes his seat, and
picks up the phone.

                    STORY TELLER (V.O.)
          Even in the winter months, like
          clock work, the once-a-week
          instruction continued. The
          instructor and student were pleased
          with the progress. And the more
          Chris learned, the more he wanted to
          become an option trader.

                    CHRIS
          Looks like you've brought some
          serious reading material.

Freeman shows his book cover "Option Long & Short" to
Chris. Opens the book to an indexed page showing Row
Data and Raw Data and presses it up against the glass.

                    FREEMAN
          I wrote this book a while ago. There
          is a section in it on Row Data and
          Raw Data, the important elements in
          my option theory. To be a successful
          Options Trader, you need to study
          both.

                    CHRIS
          My inmate teacher never talked about
          Cycle Option and Row and Raw Data.
          So why is it so important?

                    FREEMAN
          Why? Because option trading is
          speculative and the more information
          you have the better you can make the
          right strategy. I'll leave this book
          for you.

                    CHRIS
If I haven't said it before, I'll
say it now. Thank you Sir, for
visiting every week and for being
such a good teacher.

                    FREEMAN
From what Biyu told me about you and
having spent time with you here,
It's my pleasure as well.

                    CHRIS
Here it is impossible to get the
data you mentioned today. My only
other source would be Biyu, and even
for her it would not be easy.

                    FREEMAN
Biyu has always been your great
supporter, I'll give her guidance on
how to help you.

                    CHRIS
Thank you, Sir. You've turned my
life around. For that, I'll always
be grateful.

                    FREEMAN
I'm happy to experience in teaching
in Stanley Prison.

Freeman gives Chris a satisfied smile.

INT. CHRIS'S PRISON CELL - NIGHT

Chris reads from Freeman's book "Options Long & Short",
highlighting and makings notes on the book.

INT. BIYU'S SMALL FLAT - NIGHT

Notebook showing an Excel file named "Raw Data Report".

Biyu is carefully studying stock option daily market
reports, collecting the changes of open interest into
excel, and completes the file.

Some envelopes with stamps and the same address:
Stanley Prison, 99 Tung Tau Wan Road, Stanley, HK.
Attention: Chris Lin / 275490.

Biyu prints the Raw Data, folds them into an envelope,
and seals it.

> BIYU
> (looking at the
> envelope)
> Make money! My darling.

> STORY TELLER (V.O.)
> Because of the European Debt Crises
> in 2011, the stock market took a
> gigantic hit. With Biyu's assistance
> keep sending Raw Data information to
> Chris, the jailed options trader,
> made a handsome profit and realized
> this is the business he would work
> on for the rest of his life.

INT. PRISON WARDEN'S OFFICE - DAY

The Warden, a British officer, follows the copy of the
letter from Freeman to the Correctional Services
Department.

> STORY TELLER (V.O.)
> Just before Christmas, a letter from
> Freeman To, Chris's teacher, to the
> Correctional Services Department,
> pleads early release for Chris Lin
> from Stanley Prison.

INT. PRISON PERSONAL BELONGINGS HOLDING AREA - DAY

> STORY TELLER (V.O.)
> Freeman To in his letter convinced
> the officer that the prisoner 275490
> Chris Lin would no longer traffic
> drugs or be involved in any shady
> business. He had found a legitimate
> endeavor that would set him up for
> life. As the result, Chris Lin was
> released from Stanley Prison three
> months early.

Chris picks up his personal belongings and gets a copy of his receipt from the Prison Guard store keeper.

EXT. STANLEY PRISON GATES - EARLY MORNING

Title: "Stanley Prison, Christmas 2013"

Biyu waits for Chris's release.

With the gate closing behind him, Chris rushes to embrace the love of his life. He carries a bag with a lot of letters and the toy pig.

They fall into each other's arms in a passionate embrace.

> BIYU
> I waited for you with no thoughts ever thinking of others.

> CHRIS
> This is the second-most happiest day of my life.

> BIYU
> The first being?

> CHRIS
> Picking up a young girl who fell off her bike when she tried to run me over.

> BIYU
> And I am so happy you did. Let's get you cleaned up, dressed up and looking like the man I fell in love with.

MONTAGE: CHRIS AND BIYU'S LOVE STORY (REPRISE)

Scenes extracted from their first dating dinner in an upscale restaurant, the piano concert at Hong Kong City Hall, the night at the sea-view room at Gold Coast Hotel.

INT. BARBER SHOP - DAY

Chris gets a shave and a haircut.

> STORY TELLER (V.O.)
> Ten years of jail vanished in a
> matter of hours, under Biyu's
> supervision, Chris rejuvenated.

EXT. SHOPPING MALL - DAY

Chris and Biyu enters a grand shopping mall.

MONTAGE: BUYING A NEW OUTFIT FOR CHRIS

Chris and Biyu buying a new outfit from shoes and socks
to underwear, pants, jacket, shirt, and tie. Mugging it
up as they do.

> STORY TELLER (V.O.)
> Together again, the shopping spree
> ignited passions from years ago when
> as teenagers their love first
> bloomed and good time memories were
> made.

INT. SHOPPING MALL WASHROOM - DAY

Chris changes his old shabby clothes from years ago and
dons his new outfit from underwear to outerwear. He
then throws all his old clothes into the rubbish bin.
Looking at his receipt from the prison store keeper,
Chris tears it up and flushes it down the toilet.

> CHRIS
> (speaks to himself with
> SF of flushing)
> My stupid past ends here and gone
> with the drain.

Chris looks at the toilet, watching the drain.

Chris exits the washroom all dressed up and looking
fine.

>   BIYU
> As handsome as ever. Maybe even more
> so. Just like the man I fell in love
> with more than a decade.

They embrace emotionally.

>   BIYU (cont'd)
> I need to make a take-out food stop
> on the way home.

>   CHRIS
> Like real food for a change?

>   BIYU
> Yes, real food.

INT. BIYU'S SMALL FLAT/FRONT DOOR - DAY

Chris carries the bag of fast food as Biyu unlocks the
front door. They enter.

INT. BIYU'S SMALL FLAT/FRONT HALL - DAY (CONTINUOUS)

>   BIYU
>   (calling out)
> John, I'm home.

JOHN LIN, an 8-year-old boy about 130cm high, wears a
Santa Hat as he runs down the hall to greet his mother.

>   JOHN LIN
> Mommy you're home.

>   BIYU
> And your father has brought food for
> you.

>   JOHN LIN
> My father? He has come home?

>   BIYU
> Yes. Your father is home at last.

>   CHRIS
> Oh my God, I have a son?

                    BIYU
          Yes, he is your beautiful son!

Chris, holding John's face and kisses his forehead,
starts tearing. Then he wraps John and Biyu with his
arms, 3 of them are in tears.

Beat.

Chris raises up his head.

                    CHRIS
               (emotionally)
          This is my promise, I'll give all of
          my love and good life for this
          family. Forever!

                    JOHN LIN
          Forever? Father?

                    CHRIS
          Yes! Forever!

INT. BIYU'S SMALL FLAT/BEDROOM - SUNRISE

After a night of passion they awake, cuddled up.

                    STORY TELLER (V.O.)
          10 years of celibacy ended on their
          first night together. Once again,
          the passionate expression of love
          they shared years before, made Chris
          and Biyu complete.

Caressing Biyu's hair.

                    CHRIS
          Every night I fell asleep dreaming I
          was holding my Jasper precious stone
          in my arms. It helped keep me alive.

                    BIYU
          And every night I fell asleep
          knowing someday we would be together
          again and never part. Before we were
          two. Now we are one.

As they embrace,

                    CHRIS
          Yes, we are one now.

EXT. OPEN-AIR BAR - EVENING (SYDNEY, AUSTRALIA)

Title: "Sydney, Christmas 2013"

In an open-air music lounge, Oliver, Chris's prison
friend and option teacher, is enjoying the Happy Hour
with his FRIENDS. His cell phone is ringing, his free
hand cupped to his other ear to drown out the BAND that
is just finishing a set.

                    OLIVER
          Who's calling me during happy hour
          and cutting into my party time?

INT. BIYU'S SMALL FLAT - AFTERNOON

                    CHRIS
          Oliver it's me Chris. Can you hear
          me?

INTERCUT phone conversation with open-air bar, Sydney,
Australia

                    OLIVER
          Who?

                    CHRIS
          Oliver it's me Chris. Chris calling.

Oliver walking away from the band.

                    OLIVER
          Hold on a minute while I put some
          distance between me and the music.
          Who did you say you are again?

                    CHRIS
          Prisoner 275490 aka Chris Lin.

                    OLIVER
          Oh my God. It's you Chris! You're
          out? No more brown suits and lousy
          food?

CHRIS
Yes, and as free as a bird now.

Oliver walking back to the band and covering the phone
mouthpiece, he makes a request to SUSAN the pretty
Chinese girl violin player in the band.

OLIVER
Hold on. I've got a memory for you.

Calling the violin player to the front of the stage.

OLIVER (cont'd)
Can you play a song for my friend in
Hong Kong?

Oliver whispers the title and holds his cell phone up
to the violin player.

SUSAN
Sure!

As she starts to play, Chris from the phone recognizes
Auld Lang Syne, the same song played when they met in
the Stanley yard.

OLIVER
I could play it myself, but I gave
my harmonica to a friend a few years
ago.

CHRIS
I still have it and play it almost
as good as you.

OLIVER
Hold on, let me thank the pretty
musician, be right back.

Oliver puts fifty Australian Dollars in the pocket of
Susan Lee's vest.

SUSAN
Thank you! Anytime, any tune, just
give me a shout.

OLIVER
My friend in Hong Kong thanks you as
well.

Giving Oliver that patented come-on-sweet-girl smile,
she walks back to the band, stops to look at Oliver
watching her. A connection has been made.

                    CHRIS
          Hey buddy, I'm paying for this call.
          You still there.

                    OLIVER
          Sorry. Got distracted for a minute.
          Still here.

                    CHRIS
          I remember that day, the song, my
          good friend and teacher. A lot of
          things from my past pop into my head
          at the strangest of times.

                    OLIVER
          When is a good time to chat?

                    CHRIS
          Name it and I'll be there.

                    OLIVER
          How about same time tomorrow? I'll
          be at home. Easier to talk then.

                    CHRIS
          Good, we can catch up. Someone's
          knocking on my door. Let's talk
          tomorrow.

INT. BIYU'S SMALL FLAT/DOORWAY - AFTERNOON (CONTINUOUS)

Hanging up his phone, Chris answers the door to reveal
Ah Chan.

                    CHRIS
          What the fuck are you doing here.

                    AH CHAN
          What's it been? 10 long years,
          Chris?
               (pushing his way inside)
          Remember our deal? You still owe me
          money and now you owe me favors.

                    CHRIS
        I just got out of prison and don't
        have any money right now.

                    AH CHAN
        Then pay with a favor. Something
        really easy where you don't have to
        do a thing?

                    CHRIS
        Like what?

                    AH CHAN
        I have a friend who owns a luxury
        night club and is looking for a
        receptionist to entertain big
        spenders.

                    CHRIS
        What's that got to do with me?

                    AH CHAN
        It's not about you. It's about your
        pretty woman. If she works the club
        two nights a week for three months
        and I write off what you owe. Deal?

Beat.

Emotionally Chris grabs a table knife with his right
hand, and pushes Ah Chan towards the opened door by
seizing his jacket tightly with his left hand, waves
the knife at Ah Chan's head cutting him on the back of
his neck.

                    CHRIS
                (cold and calculated)
        Any dirty ideas to do or threaten my
        family, I'll kill you for sure! Pay
        you back within 3 months, fuck off!

Brandishing the knife, Chris pushes him out off the
door.

Chris slams the door and clam himself down.

                    CHRIS (cont'd)
        Now let the fuck out of my life.

EXT. BIYU'S SMALL FLAT - AFTERNOON (CONTINUOUS)

Returning home from grocery shopping, Biyu sees Ah Chan exiting their apartment building and holding his neck.

> STORY TELLER (V.O.)
> Watching the evil, the money lending
> drug dealer, leave their apartment
> building, terrifying memories from
> ten years ago flashing through
> Biyu's mind.

INT. BIYU'S SMALL FLAT/BATHROOM - AFTERNOON (CONTINUOUS)

Chris washes the blood from the knife.

INT. BIYU'S SMALL FLAT/FRONT HALL - AFTERNOON (CONTINUOUS)

Chris returns the cleaned knife to the hall table. The front door opens as Biyu enters with her groceries.

> BIYU
> Oh my dear, on my way home, I saw
> the drug dealer leaving our
> building. Please tell me he's not
> back in your life.

Taking the groceries from Biyu, Chris puts them on the table where the knife sits. In contrast to his violent action with Ah Chan, he embraces Biyu and caresses her hair.

> CHRIS
> (tenderly)
> Nothing to worry about my precious
> stone. I took care of it.
> Everything's just fine now.

Holding Biyu close and gently caressing her.

> STORY TELLER (V.O.)
> Having permission from Biyu's
> parents to marry Chris, it is the
> time to make this family recognized.

INT. HONG KONG MARRIAGE REGISTRY OFFICE - DAY

Chris and Biyu sit in the first row, John, Lin Tailor and his wife Ting Ting, with Dr. Song and Mrs. Song in the second row.

MARRIAGE OFFICIAL conducting the ceremony.

> MARRIAGE OFFICIAL
> I will ask each of you to read the oath of marriage and then everyone can sign the marriage certificate.

Handing over Biyu and Chris a card with the marriage oath on it.

> CHRIS
> I call upon all persons here present to witness that I, Chris Lin, do take you, Biyu Scarlet Song, as my lawful wedded wife.

> BIYU
> I call upon all persons here present to witness that I, Biyu Scarlet Song, do take you, Chris Lin, as my lawful wedded husband.

> MARRIAGE OFFICIAL
> Please sign the marriage certificate, and your guests as well.

> CHRIS
> For years, my heart has longed for the moment my precious jade would be my wife.

Chris opens the ring box, to reveal a pair of Jade rings. Chris places the Lady's ring on Biyu's finger and Biyu places Gent's ring on Chris finger.

> BIYU
> And you my husband for choosing me. In the eyes of our parents and son, now we really are one.

PHOTOGRAPHER is taking pictures of the newly wedded couple and the happy parents as well as John.

EXT. BICYCLE PATH NEAR THE SEASHORE - DAY (YEARS LATER)
(CONTINUOUS)

Photographer takes more pictures of Chris and Biyu with
a bicycle.

INT. CHRIS AND BIYU'S HOME - DAY

Chris, Biyu and John look through a photo album of
their wedding pictures. "Thank you for picking me up
and choosing me" is the title under the first bicycle
picture.

>   STORY TELLER (V.O.)
> Returning to the place their journey
> began, the memory of that day on the
> bicycle path was now on record in
> the family album.

>   JOHN LIN
> Why are these pictures with a
> bicycle?

>   BIYU
> If you ask me or your father, you'll
> get different answers.

>   JOHN LIN
> Father, why is there a bicycle in
> this picture?

>   CHRIS
> Your mother tried to run me over
> with her bicycle. That's how we met.

>   JOHN LIN
> Really?

>   BIYU
> Not really. He was walking on the
> bicycle path. I rang my bell many
> times and he would not get out of my
> way.

>   JOHN LIN
> But it says here, "Thank you for
> picking me up and choosing me".

                    BIYU
          I fell off my bicycle and hurt my
          knee. Your father picked me up and
          walked me home.

                    JOHN LIN
          What about "choosing me"?

                    CHRIS
          I wondered how I could meet the girl
          of my dreams and there she was at my
          feet. Choosing your mother was one
          of the best things I've ever done in
          my life.

                    JOHN LIN
          All because of a bicycle accident?

                    CHRIS
          Yes, all because of a bicycle
          accident.

                    JOHN LIN
          Wow!

Chris leaves the parlor to go to bedroom while Biyu and
John continue to look at the pictures.

INT. CHRIS AND BIYU'S HOME/BEDROOM - DAY (CONTINUOUS)

Seating on the edge of the bed, Chris punches some
numbers into the table phone and waits.

INT. AH CHAN'S SMALL CRAMPED FLAT - DAY (CONTINUOUS)

Ah Chan picks up his phone.

                    AH CHAN
          Hello.

INTERCUT phone conversation with Chris and Biyu's home/
bedroom.

>   CHRIS
> Ah Chan, it's not quite three months
> but tomorrow I'll deposit to your
> bank account the money I owe, pay in
> full. Same Hong Kong Bank account?

>   AH CHAN
> Yes, it is. If you can afford to pay
> me in full now, your wife must be
> very proud of you and your success.

>   CHRIS
> I told you before, leave my family
> out of this or I will kill you.
> Fuck!

INT. CHRIS AND BIYU'S HOME/BEDROOM - DAY (CONTINUOUS)

Chris violently slams the phone down. The sound
startles Biyu in.

>   BIYU (O.S.)
> Are you alright my love?

>   CHRIS
> Everything is just fine.

INT. HONG KONG AIRPORT ARRIVAL HALL - DAY

Title: "Chinese New Year 2014"

>   STORY TELLER (V.O.)
> Just before Chinese New Year in 2014
> Oliver and his fiancee Susan Lee
> returned to Hong Kong to meet her
> parents in China, announce their
> plans to get married and catch up
> with his old friend Chris and his
> family.

The Lin family wait to greet Chris's old friend and
teacher.

>   CHRIS
>   (anxious)
> We haven't seen each other since
> prison, and that was years ago.
>   (MORE)

> CHRIS (cont'd)
> How do I say thank you to the man
> who changed my life?

> BIYU
> Easy. Give him a big man-to-man hug
> and say thank you for changing my
> life.

Oliver and Susan Lee exit customs and immigration, bags
in hand.

> CHRIS
> I think that's them. Oliver, over
> here.

Oliver waves back as Chris hurries to meet him. They
embrace in a mano-to-mano bear hug.

> CHRIS (cont'd)
> How many years has it been my
> friend?

> OLIVER
> Too many but here we are now and I'm
> happy for that.

Oliver shaking hands with Biyu and John.

> OLIVER (cont'd)
> Biyu, it's wonderful we're here now.
> I'll never forget how you helped us
> in jail to run the small money
> option trading.
>
> Let me introduce, this is my fiancee
> Susan Lee. She's the violinist that
> played the song over the phone. We
> came to get blessing from her
> parents for our marriage. And to see
> my old friends.

Chris shaking hands with Susan.

> CHRIS
> Susan, I am so happy that you will
> marry him because of playing the
> song for me.
> (MORE)

                    CHRIS (cont'd)
          But in Stanley Prison I predicted
          Oliver will marry a Chinese girl
          because he asked me to teach him
          Chinese as our first deal.

All of them are laughing.

                    CHRIS (cont'd)
          This is my wife Biyu, she saved my
          life.

Biyu shaking with Susan and giving embraces, the two
women size each other up.

                    JOHN LIN
          Mum, you play piano, Dad plays
          harmonica, and Auntie Susan plays
          violin.

                    CHRIS
          But uncle Oliver is a master at
          playing harmonica. That's how we
          met.

                    JOHN LIN
          Wow!

                    BIYU
          My son John is learning piano from
          me, and now I am a piano teacher
          after Chris's release.

                    SUSAN
          And I play in a stage band in
          Australia, that's how I met Oliver.

                    BIYU
          Someday I'll tell you how I met my
          husband and how he picked me up.

                    CHRIS
          Girls talk. You got to love it. I'll
          get the car. Meet you at the curb.

They exit the terminal.

> STORY TELLER (V.O.)
> Susan and Oliver, the honey couple
> after having the blessing from
> parents, they returned to Australia.

INT. CHRIS AND BIYU'S HOME - EVENING

Biyu gives John a lesson on their upright piano in the parlor while in the adjoining study, Chris pours over a chart, studying Row data and Raw data and Option Quotations.

> BIYU
> Practice, practice, practice. That's
> what makes a good piano player. To
> be a great piano player you have to
> have soul and feel the music. I'm
> going to talk to your father, but
> I'll be listening.

Biyu moves to the study desk while John Lin practises a classical song. A dual time desk clock shows Hong Kong time at 8pm and Sydney time at 11 pm.

Chris on a phone call to Oliver.

> CHRIS
> How about we establish a fund to
> trade options and make more real
> money?

> OLIVER (V.O.)
> I've been thinking much the same. I
> have sources for funding. But you
> need to have a licence in order to
> trade and it's not easy to pass the
> exam. You up for that?

> CHRIS
> More now than ever before. Hey, the
> love of my life just walked in. Talk
> later. Bye.

Hanging up the phone as Biyu walks in. Biyu, pregnant, is standing behind her husband, she massages his neck and shoulders.

On Chris desk, the dual monitors, one is showing the
Stock chart and another showing an Excel file of Raw
Data Report.

              BIYU
      Did I hear you talking to Oliver?

              CHRIS
      Yes my love. We're thinking of
      starting a business of trading
      option with other people's money.

              BIYU
      With the abilities of you and
      Oliver, why not? It's a good idea.
      You have the talent to achieve great
      things you wish, I know you can.

              CHRIS
        (enjoying a neck
        massage)
      Oliver says he has a network of
      financial resources, that will help
      to look for a job and also fund for
      Option trade. But, I must take the
      exam to get the licence first, once
      I do, we're in business.

              BIYU
        (holding Chris face
        from his back and
        kisses his forehead)
      So do it! My dear! Go ahead to
      prepare the exam, I will take care
      of the Raw Data works for you.

MONTAGE: CHRIS STUDYING HARD

Chris studies for his financial licence day and night.
Biyu helps him preparing the option Raw Data.

            STORY TELLER (V.O.)
      With the support of his wife, Oliver
      and Freeman, Chris studied hard with
      a commitment not found since his
      early prison days.

             (MORE)

>   STORY TELLER (V.O.) (cont'd)
> Every spare moment, day or night,
> Chris would pour over regulation
> books, preparatory courses, and
> internet searches.
>
> Preparing for his licence exam,
> Chris was consumed by learning all
> he could.

INT. CHRIS AND BIYU'S HOME/STUDY AREA - NIGHT

Chris opens and reads his rejection letter from the
Authority. Biyu and John Lin beside him for support.

>   CHRIS
>   (tearing up the letter
>   silently)
> I must try my utmost again!

>   STORY TELLER (V.O.)
> His first attempt failed but rather
> than give up, he became even more
> energized. He promised he would not
> fail again. On the second attempt,
> he passed.

Chris hanging his exam certificate on his study wall.
Biyu and John Lin beaming.

>   JOHN LIN
> Father, you are so happy, this paper
> must be important to you.

>   CHRIS
> Yes, it certainly is, you will know
> soon.

INT. TAILOR SHOP - DAY

Lin Tailor measures Chris, Ting Ting chooses a fabric.

>   LIN TAILOR
> You are applying a good job and a
> good job needs a good suit. Clothes
> make the man.

                    CHRIS
          The first time you made me a suit,
          was for my date with Biyu, now she
          is my wife. This time is for my
          first real job, I will make it.
          Thank you father and thank you
          mother.

                    TING TING
          Don't be too proud in your
          interview. The girl liked you in
          your new suit but this time your
          boss might not be as impressed.

                    CHRIS
          I promise to make all of you proud.
          And this is just the beginning.

EXT. INVESTMENT BANK BUILDING - DAY

Chris in his new suit pauses to look at the company
sign before entering.

INT. INVESTMENT BANK HUMAN RESOURCES OFFICE - DAY

Chris is interviewed by a 50-year-old AMERICAN WOMAN
HUMAN RESOURCES MANAGER.

                    H.R. MANAGER
          Your resume is quite impressive. You
          have solid trade experience, and the
          necessary certification, but in all
          my years in the H.R. business, I've
          never had someone list being in
          prison on their applications.

                    CHRIS
          It's a rule by the Correctional
          Services Department that I have to
          follow. That was long ago and cost
          me many years of my life. Now I see
          it as an investment. A life
          opportunity.

                    H.R. MANAGER
          Duly noted. And that is why Mr.
          Oliver Cooper recommended you to us.

                    CHRIS
          Oliver, yes, he was the inmate in
          Stanley Prison.

                    H.R. MANAGER
          He notified us of your talent some
          time ago. Said you were a very good
          option trader and eager to start a
          new life.

                    CHRIS
          He was my option teacher in prison
          and now my friend in life.

                    H.R. MANAGER
          Give me a few days to review your
          application and I'll contact you
          with my decision.

                    CHRIS
          Thanks a lot! I will treasure this
          opportunity.

H.R. manager puts Chris's resume in a folder.

                    H.R. MANAGER
          Good Luck! Young man.

INT. CHRIS'S SMALL OFFICE - DAY

Title: "Easter 2015"

Oliver and Susan Lee admire the name plate on Chris's
desk. It reads, Chris Lin -- Fund Manager.

                    OLIVER
          Well mister big, you finally made
          it.

                    SUSAN
          Time to take a victory lap. How
          about dinner later this week to
          celebrate?

                    OLIVER
               (teasing)
          Bring your wife. The lady who
          deserves better than you.

SUSAN
Speaking of victory laps, do you
know what's happening to the China
stock market these days? We're just
back from China, a lot of people are
getting into the market crazily on
margin, very very high leverage.

OLIVER
It's like the U.S. in 2008. People
who can't afford to buy houses are
doing it anyway and going deep in
debt.
(knocks on Chris's desk)
It's got to be creating a huge
bubble and an opportunity to make
some big money if it's played right.

Chris is checking the chart of Shanghai-A shares
immediately.

CHRIS
To play it right means making a
Short position.

OLIVER
Yes, Long Put index, Long Call and
Short Futures, Short Call over-
valued stocks, naked. Play them all
the right way bit by bit and we'll
make real big money.

CHRIS
Noted, it is an opportunity, let me
think about and make a plan.
(turns to Susan)
Susan, you have a lot of contacts in
the Mainland, I would like you to
work for this fund to recruit more
investors from China, how do you
both think?

OLIVER
Oh, it is a good idea, isn't?

SUSAN
Yes, sound interesting, I am happy
to try, but my violin time will be
less by then.

INT. CHRIS'S SMALL OFFICE - DAY

Title: "August 2015"

From his office, Chris speaks to his partner Oliver and reports their good fortune.

>   CHRIS
> Hi Buddy. Did you notice the market
> has dropped more than twenty
> percent?

>   OLIVER
> Lucky man you are. Keep holding.

INT. HONG KONG AIRPORT BOARDING AREA - DAY

Title: "Hong Kong International Airport, October 10, 2015.

Oliver and Chris are checking the flight information board for their Cathay Pacific flight to New York.

>   STORY TELLER (V.O.)
> Invited to a meeting with the
> company CEO in New York, Oliver and
> Chris believe this Investment Bank
> is planning to expand the Option
> fund in Hong Kong and China markets.
>
> The two partners will play a big
> role in moving the fund forward. As
> it turned out, they were right.

They are sitting in the boarding area.

>   CHRIS
> It will be a successful journey, how
> do you think?

>   OLIVER
> Yes, sure! We need to have more
> OPM - other people's money to make
> the fund bigger. It is always what
> the bosses wanted.

They stand up and queue for boarding.

                    OLIVER (cont'd)
          But the more money you run the more
          problem you have. You will know, my
          buddy.

INT. CHRIS AND BIYU'S UPSCALE APARTMENT/STUDY CORNER –
NIGHT

Title: "Christmas 2015"

Chris and Oliver are in a verbal fight. Biyu and Susan
standing next to the baby grand piano watching about
one-year-old KIMBERLY sitting in her baby stroller,
listening to the heated conversation.

                    OLIVER
          I tell you Chris, the market has
          reversed, our positions can't last.
          It's the time to get out! If we
          don't, we'll lose our bread in the
          mouth.

                    CHRIS
          Sorry, I think you're wrong. What's
          happening is just a rebound but not
          a trend change. We should keep
          holding for a while longer. My gut
          tells me so.

INT. CHRIS AND BIYU'S UPSCALE APARTMENT/PARLOR – NIGHT
(CONTINUOUS)

As the animated argument continues in the background,
Biyu and Susan sitting on the piano bench with the
magazine of bridal gowns open and upright on the music
rack. Each with a glass of wine in their hand.

                    OLIVER (O.S.)
          I'm telling you I'm not about to
          lose money. So now what Mister Big?

                    SUSAN
          And these guys are friends?

                    BIYU
          Imagine if they hated each other.
          What happens next? Throwing dishes?

                    SUSAN
      If they don't calm down soon, we'll
      have to put on some girly charm, and
      rescue them from themselves.

INT. CHRIS AND BIYU'S UPSCALE APARTMENT/STUDY CORNER -
NIGHT (CONTINUOUS)

                    CHRIS
      Here's the deal, if we lose I eat
      the loss, if we win you keep your
      winning share. This way you are a
      winner no matter what happens. Deal?

                    OLIVER
      Okay! I'll take your offer.

The women enter the study corner to charm the
combatants and calm the men down.

INT. CHRIS'S SMALL OFFICE - DAY

A series of charts showing the market's deep drop in
Jan 2016 and then continuing to rise.

                    STORY TELLER (V.O.)
      As it turned out, early 2016 was a
      very good money maker. They made
      quite a haul on Chris's gut feeling
      and no dishes were ever broken in
      the process. The student had bested
      the teacher and once again, all was
      well.

Sitting on the Boss chair, Chris is showing his
confidence and pride.

                    STORY TELLER (V.O.) (cont'd)
      As suggested by Chris, Susan starts
      working in the fund, with the
      financial knowledge from Oliver, she
      has done a good job, recruited many
      wealthy investors from Mainland
      China. Business is excellent and so
      as life.

INT. OLIVER'S HOME - NIGHT

Oliver is watching a harmonica box sit on a side table and opens it, showing a harmonica which is the same model as he gave to Chris when he was released from Stanley.

> OLIVER
> (holding the harmonica
> and speaks to himself)
> I was so smart to do the right thing
> in Stanley Prison.

Sitting on the sofa, with Susan Lee's head on his lap and eyes closed, Oliver casually plays the theme from Doctor Zhivago.

INT. INVESTMENT BANK OFFICE - EVENING (CHRISTMAS 2017)

A decorated Christmas tree supports a banner "Happy Christmas" and "Hong Kong 20-years' of Handover". OFFICE REVELERS and WEALTHY CHINESE CLIENTS bringing gifts, enjoy the Christmas party.

Biyu is playing Christmas songs by a high-end keyboard, GIRLS are singing together. Susan and Oliver are entertaining the clients.

GAO ZONG appears.

> RECEPTIONIST
> Hey Susan, your client Gao Zong's
> coming.

> SUSAN
> Hi Mr. Gao Zong, thanks for coming.
> It is a wonderful day, I'd like to
> introduce my husband Oliver. He is
> one of the key persons running your
> money.

> GAO ZONG
> Oh, good, the result of the
> investment is excellent. Let me
> introduce, this is my wife.

Oliver shaking hands with Mrs. Gao first, then with Gao Zong.

                    OLIVER
I'm just one part of a team working
on your account, the real brain that
drives our success is Chris Lin.
He's the best Option Trader in the
company.

                    MRS. GAO
Tell him his efforts have made us
very happy and we will continue
investing.

                    OLIVER
Mrs. Gao, I'm sure Chris would
appreciate hearing your comments
directly. Let me introduce him to
you.

Calling Chris over from a group of party people.

                    OLIVER (cont'd)
Chris, I want you to meet two of our
guests.

Chris joins Susan, Oliver, Gao Zong and his wife.

                    OLIVER (cont'd)
Chris, let me introduce Gao Zong and
his Wife.

Chris shaking hands with Mrs. Gao and Mr. Gao.

                    GAO ZONG
I was just mentioning to Oliver that
I'm very happy with my returns this
year. He says it's all because of
your Option Trading ability.

                    CHRIS
Thank you. Oliver is being modest
about his contribution to our
success here. We are a team.

                    MRS. GAO
You are excellent, I'll introduce
more of my associates to do business
with you.

                    SUSAN
        Thank you! An endorsement like that
        calls for a Champagne toast.

                    MRS. GAO
        To good health, prosperity and
        happiness.

Raising their glasses.

Biyu waiting for Freeman at the entrance.

                    BIYU
        Hi, Freeman, I'm so glad you're able
        to come. Chris must be very happy
        seeing you joining this party.

Freeman follows Biyu to the party.

                    BIYU
        Chris! Look who's here.

                    CHRIS
        Oh, To Sir, so happy to see you
        here.

Chris shaking hands with Freeman, they embrace.

                    FREEMAN
        Wow, what an unbelievable success
        you have made.

                    CHRIS
        We've done well but without your
        teaching, I don't know where I would
        be today. Let me introduce you to
        Oliver. He was my inmate teacher as
        I mentioned.

Freeman and Oliver shaking hands.

                    OLIVER
        Chris said you are the man who
        changed his life.

                    FREEMAN
        Yes, and I was also told you were
        the one who started this change.
                    (MORE)

>   FREEMAN (cont'd)
>   (pick up a glass of
>   wine from WAITER)
>   In Stanley Prison, I already smelled
>   his success today, so I wrote to the
>   jail asking for his early release.

>   OLIVER
>   Yes, tonight's celebration proves
>   you have done the right thing.
>   Cheers!

Toasting the moment.

>   CHRIS
>   Freeman, your understanding and
>   strategy of the Hong Kong Option
>   market has proven to be really
>   practical. Thank you for your
>   sharing.

>   FREEMAN
>   In the stock market, you'll never
>   know what tomorrow will be.
>   Especially if it appears too good to
>   be true. Be very cautious in the
>   coming year.

A number of happy guests are taking pictures in front
of the Christmas tree.

INT. CHRIS'S SEA-VIEW OFFICE - NIGHT

The Christmas party is over, with champagne glasses on
hand, Chris and Oliver share a moment overlooking the
Victoria Harbour.

>   OLIVER
>   What a beautiful night!

>   CHRIS
>   Yes, this is Hong Kong, I love it.

                    OLIVER
        Sure, me too. But much credit for a
        night like this, is because of our
        wives.Susan really helps a lot
        recruiting the fund from Mainland,
        this is not my ability could
        approach. And Biyu, she has been
        your champion from the very
        beginning.

                    CHRIS
        Yes, no doubt at all. I'll never
        forget her love and support when I
        was down. I have been thinking how
        to repay my precious stone for all
        she has done.

Raising their glasses.

                    OLIVER
        To Biyu and Susan.

                    CHRIS
        Yes, to our wives.

INT. CHRIS AND BIYU'S UPSCALE APARTMENT - LATE
AFTERNOON

Biyu stops playing the baby grand piano when Chris and
CLAUSE SCHNEIDER enter the flat. Chris introduces
Clause to Biyu.

                    CHRIS
        Biyu my love, I want you to meet
        Clause Schneider from Austria. He
        will be the new pianist for the Hong
        Kong Philharmonic Orchestra and has
        agreed to be your piano mentor.

A surprised Biyu stands up to greet her new mentor.

                    BIYU
        Really? Who will play in the
        Philharmonic Orchestra and will be
        my piano mentor?

                    CHRIS
          Yes, my dear precious stone. I've
          been thinking about this for a long
          time. I really want to do something
          to compensate your love.

Chris kisses Biyu.

Clause shaking Biyu's hand.

                    CLAUSE SCHNEIDER
          Your first love told me the piano
          has always been your second love.

                    BIYU
          Thank you for the kind words Mister
          Schneider.

                    CLAUSE SCHNEIDER
          Both of you, call me Clause please.
          May I share your bench, Mrs. Lin,
          and listen to you play some more?

                    BIYU
          Sure!

Clause sits beside Biyu.

                    CHRIS
          If you'll excuse me, I'll open a
          bottle of wine to celebrate your
          first lesson. I'll be listening.

Chris leaves for the dining room as Biyu opens her
exercise book and chooses Marriage d'Amour.

                    CLAUSE SCHNEIDER
          An excellent choice, Mrs. Lin.

Biyu starts to play and Clause plays the accompaniment.

INT. CHRIS AND BIYU'S UPSCALE APARTMENT/DINING ROOM -
LATE AFTERNOON (CONTINUOUS)

Chris pours a glass of wine and listens to the music
from the parlor. He nods his head in approval.

INT. INVESTMENT BANK RECEPTION DESK - DAY

On the wall, there is a calendar showing January 2018.

The RECEPTIONIST buzzes Chris's office on the intercom to announce a visitor. Ah Chan and his son, ALEX CHAN, are waiting to be invited in.

> RECEPTIONIST
> There is a Mister Ah Chan and his son here to see you. He says he's an old friend and in need of your help.

INT. CHRIS'S SEA-VIEW OFFICE - DAY.

Chris sits behind his desk, phone to his ear as he listens.

INTERCUT phone conversation with office reception

> CHRIS
> Who did you say he is? His name again please.

> RECEPTIONIST
> Mr. Ah Chan and his son.

> CHRIS
> Did he say what he wants?

> RECEPTIONIST
> Something about his son. Should I send them away?

Beat.

> CHRIS
> No. No. A ghost from the past and in a weird way helped me start my business. Send them in.

> RECEPTIONIST
> Down the hall to the corner office on the left. He will see you now.

> AH CHAN
> Thank you.

INT. CHRIS'S SEA-VIEW OFFICE - DAY

Ah Chan knocks on the door. Chris waves him and his son
Alex in. They take the seats opposite to Chris's desk.

> CHRIS
> Now this is a real surprise, and
> then some.

> AH CHAN
> Because of our past relationship, it
> was not easy for me to come here.
> For the sake of my son, I knew I
> must.

> CHRIS
> What do you want?

> AH CHAN
> Let him come here and learn with
> you, so he can have a good life.

Alex Chan stands up, bows, and clasps his hands.

> ALEX CHAN
> Thank you Uncle Chris for seeing us.
> Please give me a chance to be your
> apprentice.

Chris gestures for Alex to sit down.

> CHRIS
> What happened to the old life?

> AH CHAN
> It's regulated by the government and
> I lost most of the usurer business.

> CHRIS
> No more drug king at the mechanic's
> shop?

> AH CHAN
> No more! Now I hope my son can be a
> man like you and have a better life.

Beat.

                    CHRIS
          Your visit reminds me of myself many
          years ago. Redemption is not easy to
          come by, but for your son it's a
          different story.

Chris seriously looking at Alex.

                    CHRIS (cont'd)
          Alex, nothing is easy, neither
          passing the exams for a licence to
          trade nor mastering your skills for
          a living. It will take years, I am
          going to draft a learning path for
          you later.

Alex standing up and bow to Chris.

                    ALEX CHAN
          Thank you very much! Uncle Chris.

INT. CHRIS AND BIYU'S UPSCALE APARTMENT - AFTERNOON

Chris enters home and finds John playing games on his
phone lying on sofa.

                    CHRIS
          Isn't it your piano practice time?

                    JOHN LIN
          Yes, father, but I have no desire to
          play music right now.

                    CHRIS
          Why's that?

                    JOHN LIN
          I failed my math exam and I'm
          worried I've disappointed you.

Chris sits beside John on the sofa, puts his hand on
John's head.

Beat.

> CHRIS
> A very famous man who led the
> British as the Prime Minister
> through World War II said, "Success
> is not final, failure is not fatal.
> It is the courage to continue that
> counts." That was Winston Churchill
> many years ago.

> JOHN LIN
> And that means?

Chris, face-to-face with John, shares an intimate
moment with his son.

> CHRIS
> It means you keep trying and don't
> give up. That's the courage he was
> talking about.

> JOHN LIN
> And this is a famous man?

> CHRIS
> Yes, he is very famous, you will
> meet him in history books. As you
> knew that, I failed my licence exam
> the first time, but I refused to
> give up.

> JOHN LIN
> Yes, I remember you passed in the
> second exam and were very happy.

> CHRIS
> Yes, just like Mister Churchill
> said, it's the courage to continue
> that counts. And you know what?

> JOHN LIN
> What?

> CHRIS
> You should learn harder, in the next
> math exam, I'm sure you'll pass with
> honors.

> JOHN LIN
> You won't be angry with me?

                    CHRIS
          Not at all, as long as you keep
          trying. The same is true for your
          piano practice. Now play a song for
          me please and make your mother and I
          proud of your talent.

A relieved John sits on the piano bench, begins to play
as Chris relaxes on the sofa and closes his eyes.

INT. CHRIS'S SEA-VIEW OFFICE - DAY

Title: "January 2018"

Chris paces back and forth behind his desk while Oliver
studies a chart of the Dow Jones Industrial Average.

                    CHRIS
               (to the computer)
          The correction of the Hong Kong
          market is beginning, but I think it
          can't last. 32000 points on the Hang
          Seng Index should be a support
          compared with Dow Jones.

                    OLIVER
          America had a 55% share of the
          global finance market. In 2013, Dow
          Jones recovered from the drop in
          2008-2009. Now a rising trend is
          happening, and it looks like it will
          continue.

Chris checks the Hang Seng Index chart.

                    CHRIS
          The Hang Seng Index recovered from
          that drop 5 years later than the Dow
          Jones, so the 32000 should be a
          support to rise from.

                    STORY TELLER (V.O.)
          Since 2008 when the Hang Seng Index
          dropped from 31958 to 10676, the
          Hong Kong market took 10 years to
          recover the loss, climbing over
          32000 again in 2017.

                    (MORE)

                    STORY TELLER (V.O.) (cont'd)
          But from 2018 the deep correction
          keeps moving and the market slipped
          another 5000 points.

INT. INVESTMENT BANK OFFICE HALLWAY - DAY (CONTINUOUS)

The Receptionist with a handful of phone message slips,
knocks on Chris's office door.

INT. CHRIS'S SEA-VIEW OFFICE - DAY (CONTINUOUS)

Chris gestures the receptionist to enter, on his office
wall is a clock reading 12:15.

                    RECEPTIONIST
          You look so worried, Mr. Lin.

Chris tired nodding.

                    RECEPTIONIST (cont'd)
          Here are three messages I've taken
          this morning, from clients who want
          to redeem and close their accounts.

Handing Chris the messages.

                    RECEPTIONIST (cont'd)
          All information of their portfolios
          is on their messages.

                    CHRIS
          I'll look them over and answer this
          afternoon. Thanks.

INT. ACCOUNT MANAGER OFFICE - DAY

A 50-year-old BRITISH ACCOUNT MANAGER arranges some
documents as he hurries down the hall to Chris's
office.

INT. CHRIS'S SEA-VIEW OFFICE - DAY (CONTINUOUS)

Knocking on the door, the account manager is invited
in. The wall clock now reads 4:00pm.

                    ACCOUNT MANAGER
          Chris, just the latest request to
          redeem and close account. It's from
          Gao Zong.

Chris slumps into the chair, closing his eyes.

                    ACCOUNT MANAGER (cont'd)
          If the market keeps falling, I
          expect there will be more tomorrow.
          The fund value is dropping quickly.
          We need to watch it closely.

Passing documents to Chris, he leaves.

A dazed Chris looks at the closed files on his desk.

INT. BRITISH PUB - AFTER OFFICE HOUR

Chris and Oliver plan their strategy while having a
black beer.

                    OLIVER
          I ordered black beer, I like the
          bitter taste and hope our situation
          is not as bitter. We make money, we
          lose money. All part of the
          business.

                    CHRIS
          I think I'm going to cut some
          positions instead of holding Long
          Out-of-the-Money Calls. Major
          capital should be parking on Blue
          Chips. So we can reduce our loss and
          continue to run the fund.

                    OLIVER
          Yes, it's a way to handle the
          clients. The market is jittery right
          now, and some investors are getting
          really scared.

                    CHRIS
          Like what you've said, make money
          and lose money, all part of the
          business. And the more money you
          run, the more problem you have.

EXT. STREET-SCAPE / **INT.** TRAM - NIGHT

Chris and Oliver board a tram.

> CHRIS
> I told my son something the other
> day when he was depressed. And now I
> need to tell myself the same thing.

> OLIVER
> And that is?

> CHRIS
> A quote from Winston Churchill who
> said "Success is not final, failure
> is not fatal. It is the courage to
> continue that counts."

> OLIVER
> You mean?

> CHRIS
> When times are tough, having the
> courage to continue matters most.

> OLIVER
> The ups and downs are the nature of
> this business. You just need a clear
> conscience to help them make it
> through the tough times.

Beat.

> OLIVER (cont'd)
> Are you thinking to move the capital
> to the US market?

> CHRIS
> Yes, actually we have done some. But
> no matter how bad things get, money
> we make in Hong Kong stays in Hong
> Kong. Agreed?

> OLIVER
> Agreed. Now we must convince our
> clients this is just a temporary
> setback.

> CHRIS
> We've made them a lot of money, but
> their greed is more than what we can
> imagine.

> OLIVER
> They're businessmen, so we shall
> take extra more while we are making
> more.

INT. CHRIS AND BIYU'S UPSCALE APARTMENT/HALLWAY –
EVENING

The door opens as a tired and weary Chris comes home
and relaxes on the parlor sofa.

> BIYU
> I'm going to make tea for you.

Biyu is getting up for the tea, but Chris falls asleep
on the sofa.

Biyu starts to play Marriage d'Amour slightly, with
Clause's lessons, her skill is much improved.

John returns from school, Biyu motions John to join her
at the piano and let Chris relax. Mother and Son play
very well together.

As the music continues, Chris is sleeping well.

> STORY TELLER (V.O.)
> The events of the day had left Chris
> exhausted and unhappy. Home had
> always been his safe place, his
> sanctuary. Today was no different.
> He needed it even more.

INT. CHRIS AND BIYU'S UPSCALE APARTMENT/PARLOR –
EVENING

Chris is still sleeping on sofa, Biyu, and John teaches
the 4-year-old KIMBERLY LIN (aka KIMMY) how to play a
few notes of Ode to Joy on the piano.

>   BIYU
>   Kimmy, go get your father and ask
>   him to bring his harmonica. We'll
>   make this a family affair.

Kimmy races off to get her father as Ode to Joy
continues with Biyu and John.

INT. CHRIS AND BIYU'S UPSCALE APARTMENT/PARLOR SOFA -
EVENING

Seated next him, Kimmy tugs on her father's leg.

>   KIMBERLY LIN
>   Daddy. Daddy. Mommy wants you. Bring
>   your 'monica' and play a song with
>   us. Please, Daddy.

Chris waked up and pulls Kimmy up to sit on his lap and
stroke her hair.

>   CHRIS
>   When the big princess sends the
>   little princess, how can I refuse?

Chris kisses Kimmy on her head.

>   CHRIS (cont'd)
>   See my old 'monica' over there on
>   the side table beside my toy pig?
>   Bring it, we'll join the big
>   princess and make some happy music.

INT. CHRIS AND BIYU'S UPSCALE APARTMENT/PARLOR -
EVENING

Kimmy runs to the side table, picks up the harmonica,
and pass it to Chris.

>   CHRIS
>   Never been able to say no to a
>   pretty girl especially one who looks
>   like her mother.

>   JOHN LIN
>   If she looked like you father, that
>   would be terrible.

Chris hoists Kimmy to sit on the piano bench between
Biyu and John.

>   BIYU
>   You're sounding more and more like
>   your father every day.

>   JOHN LIN
>   Time to play happy music before I
>   get in trouble.

John starts to play Ode to Joy and Kimmy with the help
of Biyu, joins in. After a couple of bars, Chris
follows with his harmonica.

Chris's spirits improve as the family playing music
together.

INT. OLIVER'S HOME - NIGHT

Lying on the sofa, Oliver is closing the eyes, his
harmonica box unopened is sitting on the side table and
aside is a glass of Whiskey. He is ignoring Susan's
attempt to comfort him.

Susan has no alternative, she opens her Violin box and
playing a beautiful serenade.

Oliver opens the eyes and smells the Whiskey, holding
the glass on hand, he enjoys Susan's music.

INT. INVESTMENT BANK OFFICE HALLWAY - DAY

A calendar showing Nov 2018.

The receptionist approaches Chris's office with a new
handful of phone messages, knocks the door and enters
the room.

INT. CHRIS'S SEA-VIEW OFFICE - DAY

>   RECEPTIONIST
>   Mr. Lin, I'm getting a lot of
>   clients' calls wanting to re-
>   activate their accounts.

Handing Chris the phone messages.

                    CHRIS
          Thanks for the good news.

The receptionist leaves as Chris looks through the
messages and smiles. Picking up the phone, he calls his
former clients.

                STORY TELLER (V.O.)
          Just before Christmas 2018, the
          market stabilized and it was back to
          business as usual. Clients who left,
          now are coming back.

Chris is calling Gao Zong.

                    CHRIS
          Gao Zong, Chris Lin calling. My
          receptionist tells me you called.
          How may I help you?

                GAO ZONG (V.O.)
          The market seems rising and I want
          to get back in before the peak. I'm
          asking you to re-activate my account
          Mister Lin. Please do.

                    CHRIS
          Thank you for renewing your
          confidence in me and the market.
          I'll re-open your account as of
          today as requested.

                GAO ZONG (V.O.)
          Thank you, Chris, I hope I'll be a
          happy man.

                    CHRIS
          As always, we'll do our best to make
          sure you are a happy man.

INT. CHRIS AND BIYU'S UPSCALE APARTMENT - EVENING

Title: "Chinese New Year 2019"

Biyu and Susan watch 5-year-old Kimmy and Susan's 3-
year-old daughter LORETTA playing in the parlor.

> SUSAN
> It's so nice for our girls to play
> and enjoy each other even if they
> are noisy.

> BIYU
> But happy noises are always welcomed
> in our home. It wasn't too long ago
> there was much sadness because
> business was bad.

> SUSAN
> I remember. Sometimes Oliver was
> hard to live with. Let's hope this
> Year of the Pig will be kind to all
> of us.

> BIYU
> A pig has always been kind to me. As
> a gift, I gave a toy one to Chris on
> our first date. It's been with us
> ever since.

> SUSAN
> It must be a love story.

> BIYU
> Yes, it's the beginning of our love.

INT. CHRIS AND BIYU'S UPSCALE APARTMENT - NIGHT

A relaxed Chris and Oliver, smoke cigars and drink red
wine at the same place they argued in 2015.

> CHRIS
> Well partner, it's been a struggle
> but now we're back.

> OLIVER
> Not a minute too soon. My moods made
> it hard for Susan to be patient with
> me.

> CHRIS
> Money is not always easy to make for
> our clients and ourselves.

In unison, they raise their glasses.

>   OLIVER
> But once again, we did it. C'est la
> vie! My friend.

STOCK FOOTAGE: HONG KONG DEMONSTRATION

Title: "June 16, 2019"

>   STORY TELLER (V.O.)
> On a hot humid day in Hong Kong, a
> historic demonstration took place as
> upwards of 2 million people gathered
> in the streets to support democracy,
> and rally against the controversial
> extradition bill.
>
> Starting at Victoria Park, thousands
> of black clothed protesters made
> their way down the 3.2 km route
> ending at Hong Kong's Parliament --
> the Legislative Council building.

EXT. CHRIS AND BIYU'S UPSCALE APARTMENT/BALCONY - DAY

The CROWD OF PROTESTERS chants "Five demands! Not one
less!"

Chris and Oliver watch the protest marching on from the
balcony.

In the front of the crowd, John dressed in black, is
seen with other emotional young students. Biyu, wearing
a first-aid vest, is on duty with Susan aside. In the
volunteers team, Alex is giving help.

Other characters in our story are seen in the crowd.

>   STORY TELLER (V.O.)
> The mass demonstration was effective
> as the extradition bill was
> temporarily suspended.

>   OLIVER
> Do you remember the book I gave you
> when I was released from Stanley
> Prison?

                    CHRIS
Sure I do. Friedman's 'Free to
Choose.' The Nobel Prize Winner for
Economics. I've read it several
times.

                    OLIVER
And how the world can be described
in two words.

                    CHRIS
Capitalism and Freedom.

                    OLIVER
Good, let's get down the streets, we
are witnessing a continuing fight
for both.

                    CHRIS
Yes, let's Long Call Hong Kong.

INT. CHRIS'S SEA-VIEW OFFICE - DAY

As the chants of 'Five Demands! Not one less!' continue
to build in volume, we see a well-used copy of Milton
Friedman's 'Free to Choose' with the harmonica and toy
pig on a table beside it. The following quotation from
the book types on the screen one letter at a time to
reveal,

"The role of competitive capitalism - the organization
of the bulk of economic activity through private
enterprise operating in a free market - is a system of
economic freedom and a necessary condition for
political freedom." -- Milton Friedman

The chants reach a deafening crescendo and end on the
dip to black.

Crew credits.

FADE OUT.

Notes

If you need help to read this movie script more smoothly, or
If you wish to receive further information about this movie script

Please send your name and mobile number to

e-mail: **thespeculators@hkoptionclass.com.hk**

Welcome to visit us at **www.hkoptionclass.com.hk**